Strengthening Nuclear Nonproliferation

Strengthening Nuclear Nonproliferation

Kathleen C. Bailey

Westview Press

BOULDER • SAN FRANCISCO • OXFORD

Copyright © 1993 by Westview Press, Inc. The U.S. Government reserves for itself and others acting on its behalf a royalty-free, nonexclusive, irrevocable, world-wide license for Governmental purposes to publish, distribute, translate, duplicate, exhibit, and perform any such data copyrighted.

Published in 1993 in the United States of America by Westview Press, Inc., 5500 Central Avenue, Boulder, Colorado 80301-2877, and in the United Kingdom by Westview Press, 36 Lonsdale Road, Summertown, Oxford OX2 7EW

Library of Congress Cataloging-in-Publication Data
Bailey, Kathleen C.
  Strengthening nuclear nonproliferation / Kathleen C. Bailey.
    p.   cm.
  Includes bibliographical references and index.
  ISBN 0-8133-2006-2. — ISBN 0-8133-2007-0 (pbk.)
  1. Nuclear nonproliferation.   I. Title.
JX1974.73.B35   1993
327.1'74—dc20

93-29169
CIP

Printed and bound in the United States of America

The paper used in this publication meets the requirements
of the American National Standard for Permanence of Paper
for Printed Library Materials Z39.48-1984.

10   9   8   7   6   5   4   3   2   1

For my father, Angus Brown Bailey

Contents

12 Conclusion **105**

Focus on Regional Conflict Resolution, 106
Widen Participation in Arms Control Agreements, 106
Military Intervention Should Be Considered, 107

Preface

I gratefully acknowledge support for this project from Lawrence Livermore National Laboratory, the United States Institute of Peace, and the National Institute for Public Policy. The opinions, findings, and conclusions or recommendations expressed in this book are mine and do not necessarily reflect the views of the United States Government or any of the above-mentioned institutions.

Many people shared their time and thoughts with me. I am indebted to the twelve experts from the International Atomic Energy Agency who briefed me on safeguards issues and to Bob Barker for taking notes and participating in the interviews.

I would like to thank several people who commented on one or more chapters: Paul Brown, Bill Domke, Bill Dunlop, Frank Houck, Joe Indusi, Neil Joeck, Steve Lambakis, Peter Lavoy, Ron Lehman, George Miller, George Moussalli, Ellen Raber, Amy Sands, Robin Staffin, Jessica Stern, Bill Sutcliff, Roland Timerbaev, and Pierre Villaros. Kristie Monica helped with typing and dozens of details. Also, Steve Peterson's and Ginny Baldwin's editing and manuscript preparation are much appreciated.

I am especially grateful to those who reviewed major portions or all of the manuscript, giving me extensive suggestions and corrections. They are George Anzelon, Paul Chrzanowski, David Fischer, Jerry Mullins, and John Simpson. The opinions expressed and any errors that these people may have missed are my own.

Kathleen C. Bailey

1

Introduction

The nuclear nonproliferation regime is a set of policies and political commitments designed since the 1960s to prevent the further spread of nuclear weapons and, to the extent possible, roll back weapons programs and pursue disarmament. The key components of the regime are treaties (both the 1968 Nuclear Nonproliferation Treaty and regional agreements), export controls (particularly the Nuclear Suppliers Group), safeguards, and bilateral and multilateral initiatives. An example of the latter is the set of UN Security Council Resolutions passed in 1991 mandating the identification and destruction of Iraq's programs for weapons of mass destruction and their delivery systems.

Since 1990, events have shown that nuclear proliferation remains a threat to world stability and security. The nuclear nonproliferation regime failed to deter or detect the Iraqi nuclear weapons program. The dissolution of the Soviet Union has created four states in possession of nuclear weapons, at least two of which have signaled intent to retain weapons status. Iran and North Korea are suspected of pursuing nuclear weapons capability, although both are party to the NPT and deny nuclear ambitions. Former Soviet nuclear weapons are being dismantled; Russia continues spent-fuel reprocessing; Japan, India, and perhaps others are amassing plutonium; Pakistan churns out enriched uranium. These activities all create an increasing pool of special nuclear materials which could be sold on the black market or stolen by terrorists. Such events pose serious challenges to the nuclear nonproliferation regime.

This book examines the components of the nuclear nonproliferation regime and policies which have been suggested as means to strengthen it. The purpose is to stimulate discussion of alternatives that might lower the likelihood of further proliferation and help reduce the nuclear arms and capabilities of proliferant states.

2

The Nuclear Nonproliferation Treaty: Purpose and Performance

Nuclear nonproliferation treaties are legal documents that provide a means for nations to make a political commitment to refrain from acquiring nuclear weapons. The Treaty of Tlatelolco and the Treaty of Rarotonga are regional treaties establishing nuclear-weapons-free zones in Latin America and the South Pacific, respectively. The Nuclear Nonproliferation Treaty (NPT)—upon which this chapter focuses— is a multilateral treaty open to membership worldwide, and has over 150 states party. These treaties cannot prevent a nation, whether a member or nonmember, from acquiring nuclear weapons if it wishes to do so. The treaties do not contain provisions for punishment of nations that choose to acquire weapons. Despite these weaknesses, the treaties have played a strong role in international nuclear nonproliferation policy. In particular, the NPT has been the basis for international discussion regarding nuclear nonproliferation and has codified norms against the spread of nuclear weapons. It has also provided a framework for NPT-type safeguards (discussed in Chapter 8) and export controls.

Because the NPT is international in scope and its norms are so widely accepted, its future is entwined in the acceptance and viability of nuclear nonproliferation as a global goal. In 1995, a conference of treaty members will meet to determine the length of time that the NPT will be extended. In a sense, the parties will be judging the performance and contribution of the NPT to the security of individual nations and the world community. This chapter reviews the purpose, weaknesses, and effectiveness of the NPT.

The Nuclear Nonproliferation Treaty

The Nuclear Nonproliferation Treaty (NPT) entered into force in 1970. It was established to help end the nuclear arms race and prevent the further spread of nuclear weapons. At the time the treaty was opened for signature in 1968, there were five existing nuclear weapons states. The United States had detonated a nuclear device in 1945; the Soviet Union, 1949; the United Kingdom, 1952; France, 1960; and China, 1964. The intent of the treaty was to stop the number at five and to commit those five to work toward disarmament. Essentially, the long-range vision of the treaty's drafters was a nuclear-weapons-free world.

To stop the number of nuclear weapons states at five, at least three major issues needed to be addressed at the outset. One was placing controls on the then rapidly expanding number of civil nuclear power programs world-wide. Civil nuclear fuel cycles can be used to generate special nuclear materials usable in explosives. Framers of the treaty sought to construct political and technical barriers to using civil nuclear industries for nonpeaceful purposes. Safeguards—inspections and monitoring of nuclear materials and facilities by an international agency—were the mainstay of the system, which was designed to prevent use of commercial and research programs for nonpeaceful purposes.

A second concern at the time was the potential transfer of nuclear weapons from a possessor state to a nonpossessor. The Soviet Union was particularly worried that the United States would transfer to or share control over nuclear weapons with its NATO allies. Ultimately, the United States solved the problem by assuring that all nuclear weapons would remain under its direct physical control. Any decision to use them would result from collective NATO decision making, and each NATO member would have veto power over the launch of a nuclear weapon from its soil.[1]

Third, the non-nuclear-weapons states, who feared that they would be militarily or economically disadvantaged by the treaty, had serious reservations. While most acknowledged the benefit of ending nuclear proliferation, they wanted assurances from the states possessing such weapons that they would work toward disarmament and would not attack or threaten to attack non-nuclear-weapons states. They also did not want to be shut out of any benefits that might accrue to possessors. For example, at the time it was widely believed that nuclear explosives—which are technically the same as weapons—were an attractive option for such peaceful activities as earth excavation.

The NPT sought to address most of the above issues. Table 1 lists its basic provisions. The record of the NPT in achieving these goals is mixed. Clearly the treaty has created a major political and diplomatic barrier to nuclear proliferation; however, some nuclear proliferation has occurred. There are a number of reasons why the treaty has not been more effective, as outlined in the paragraphs following Table 1.

TABLE 1 Basic Provisions of the NPT

- Prevent the spread of nuclear weapons.

  Article I prohibits the transfer of weapons, directly or indirectly, from states in possession of nuclear weapons. Article II disallows receipt or manufacture of weapons by non-nuclear-weapons states.

- Safeguard nuclear materials and facilities.

  Article III seeks to assure that materials and facilities in non-nuclear-weapons states are used for peaceful purposes only via application of safeguards by the International Atomic Energy Agency. All parties agree not to transfer nuclear materials and technology to these nations without arranging safeguards. (Note: Subsequently, nuclear weapons states agreed to apply safeguards to their own non-weapons-related facilities and materials.)

- Make benefits of peaceful nuclear energy available.

  Article IV assures the right of all nations to access benefits of nuclear energy. Article V specifically cites the rights of all to use peaceful nuclear explosions, under appropriate observation and procedures.

- Promote disarmament.

  Article VI commits all parties to pursue negotiations in good faith on measures to end the nuclear arms race and to achieve disarmament.

Problems with the NPT

Membership

The most serious obstacle to the treaty from the outset was nonmembership by key countries. Two acknowledged nuclear weapons states, France and China, refused to join. China did not want to participate in a treaty which it felt was inequitable. The NPT, in the Chinese view, pitted the "have" nuclear weapons states against the "have not" non-nuclear-weapons states. France did not want to antagonize Third World states and was concerned about the impact of the treaty on its nuclear-related trade and the development of its own nuclear arsenal.

Other nations that declined to join the NPT presented an even greater challenge to the nascent nonproliferation regime: the countries working to develop nuclear weapons. These countries included Israel, India, Pakistan, South Africa, Argentina, and Brazil. The first four succeeded in acquiring nuclear weapons capability and in accumulating a stockpile of special nuclear materials (plutonium or enriched uranium) for weapons purposes.

Argentina, Brazil, and South Africa subsequently took steps to dismantle their nuclear weapons programs. South Africa joined the NPT in 1992, and in March 1993 announced that it had built six nuclear weapons and subsequently destroyed them. Argentina and Brazil are working to bring into force the Treaty of Tlatelolco—the Latin American nuclear nonproliferation treaty—and have agreed to joint confidence-building measures, including safeguards. France and China both became party to the NPT. The remaining membership problem is thus centered on a few states with nuclear weapons programs: Israel, India, and Pakistan.

Noncompliance

Some nations have joined the NPT but have failed to adhere to its letter or spirit. In the 1970s, for example, three parties to the treaty—Taiwan, South Korea, and Iran—all had clandestine nuclear weapons programs in various stages of development.[2] Taiwan was pressured intensively by the United States and abandoned its effort.[3] Similar pressure was placed on South Korea. To entice Seoul to agree, the United States assuaged its security concerns by extending nuclear protection to South Korea. Iran's program was derailed by the Islamic revolution that wracked the country beginning in 1979. However, there are indications that Tehran has restarted nuclear-weapons-related activities. Former CIA Director Robert Gates stated that Iran is trying to acquire nuclear arms and could succeed in eight to ten years, given some foreign help.[4]

More recently, North Korea presented a compliance problem. Although it signed the NPT, it did not complete the safeguards agreement required by the treaty. North Korea engaged in suspicious activities, such as constructing reactors and a reprocessing facility that the government was unwilling to have inspected by the International Atomic Energy Agency (IAEA). After intense international diplomatic pressures were applied, North Korea said it would comply if a number of demands were met, including the removal of all US nuclear weaponry from South Korea. The United States later confirmed that South Korea was free of nuclear weapons.[5] That same month, December 1991, the two Koreas adopted a Joint Declaration on the Denuclearization of the Korean Peninsula, which paved the way for IAEA inspections in North Korea.

Following the IAEA inspection and analysis of samples collected at the time, the IAEA presented evidence to North Korea and the IAEA Board of Governors that North Korea had misrepresented how much and how many times plutonium had been reprocessed.[6] The IAEA again requested to inspect. North Korea responded that the site the IAEA was asking to visit was a military facility not open to IAEA inspection. Ultimately, rather than comply with the IAEA request, North Korea announced on March 12, 1993, its decision to leave the NPT. This example points out the serious problem of noncompliance, as well as the ease with which nations can legally withdraw from the treaty.

Another dramatic example of noncompliance is Iraq. Iraq's nuclear weapons program and efforts to conceal it are more thoroughly examined in Chapter 4, but here it is noted that Iraq developed a very broad-scale effort, most of which was undetected. The IAEA safeguards process did not uncover Iraq's cheating. This has raised the question whether other states might also violate the NPT without detection. The issue of verification and verifiability of the NPT is discussed in greater detail in Chapter 7.

"Haves" Versus "Have-Nots"

The NPT is inherently discriminatory in that it allows nuclear-weapons-state parties to retain their weapons while exacting a vow from non-nuclear-weapons states that they will refrain from acquiring them. Also, many nations claim that the nuclear weapons states, in their efforts to prevent proliferation, do not share the fruits of nuclear technology. This imbalance has led to contentious arguments among parties, which intensify at five-year intervals when the NPT is subject to review by its members. Generally, the debate on discrimination centers around three topics: access to nuclear technology, disarmament by the nuclear weapons states, and provision of security assurances.

Access to Technology   At the 1975 and 1980 NPT review conferences, less-developed countries were very critical of nuclear-supplier countries for failure to adequately provide nuclear energy and technology. They wanted funding for their programs, technical assistance, and freer access to full fuel-cycle technologies. To some extent, the vehemence of their demands was abetted by a few supplier countries whose commercial interests were constrained by nonproliferation policies.

In the 1980s, international interest in nuclear power began to wane as the antinuclear movement took hold. The Three-Mile Island accident in 1979 and the Chernobyl explosion and dispersal of radioactivity in 1986 severely tarnished the reputation of the nuclear industry. Perhaps of greater importance to public opinion in many developing countries, however, was an accident that had nothing directly to do with nuclear power. In Goiania, Brazil, poor people broke open a piece of dental equipment in a junkyard in 1987. Inside was cesium 137, a sparkling powder. Several people were directly exposed to it, but one little girl spread the glitter over her skin. Her agonizing death was well covered in the press, particularly in developing countries. Officials in countries as far away as India credited the disaster with alarming the public about "things nuclear."

Countries that intended to use their civil nuclear programs as the basis of a weapons program were deterred by yet another phenomenon of the 1980s: attacks against suspect nuclear facilities. In 1981, Israel bombed Iraq's nuclear reactor and support buildings at Tuwaitha, setting back the probable nuclear weapons program by a decade or so.[7] Later, during the Iran–Iraq War, Iraq bombed Iran's Bushehr reactors, which were under construction, causing the foreign personnel working on the project to abandon it. The lesson from these incidents was that a clandestine program with secret facilities, not a civil program with power reactors, might successfully survive attack.

Access to technology is still an issue to non-nuclear-weapons-state parties to the NPT. But, it has diminished in importance significantly along with the overall decline in attractiveness of civil nuclear energy.

The Disarmament Issue Non-nuclear-weapons-states party to the NPT were adamant that weapons states fulfill their Article VI obligations to work toward "cessation of the nuclear arms race" and "general and complete disarmament." In the 1980 and 1990 NPT review conferences, this issue was particularly contentious and was key to the inability to reach consensus on a final document. The context of the early and mid-1980s set the tone. The East–West arms race was intense, and there was a swirl of controversy over the deployment of intermediate nuclear forces by both sides. US and Soviet nuclear forces were increasing qualitatively and quantitatively. The Soviet Union, supported by a peace movement in the United States, was pushing hard for a "nuclear freeze" (partly to prevent international nuclear forces deployment) and an end to nuclear testing (primarily to curtail US weapons modernization).

A comprehensive test ban (CTB) and superpower disarmament were strongly supported by the nonaligned movement and its leaders, particularly India (a nonparty to the NPT). Indian leaders argued that non-nuclear-weapons states should not give up the nuclear option as long as the five acknowledged possessors held onto their own weapons. Although some confidence-building measures and arms control agreements had been negotiated by the United States and Soviet Union, it was not until late 1987 with the signing of the Intermediate Nuclear Forces Treaty (INF) that a major, effective arms reduction agreement was concluded between the two superpowers.[8] Until that time, critics of US–Soviet arms control could legitimately claim that there was nothing to reduce or roll back the arms race; efforts had only been made to limit its upper ceiling.

In the late 1980s, East–West tensions began to relax and the United States and Soviet Union continued working hard on arms control and disarmament measures, including the Strategic Arms Reduction Talks (START) and limitations on nuclear testing. The atmosphere led to decreased emphasis on "superpower disarmament" by the non-nuclear-weapons parties to the NPT.

During the preparations for the 1990 NPT Review Conference, it became clear that less-developed countries no longer focused intently on disarmament by the superpowers. In preparatory conversations prior to the 1990 review, for example, the idea of a CTB was rarely mentioned by representatives of other countries as an issue on which they would like the review to focus. In the preparations for review conferences prior to 1990, a CTB had been at the top of most countries' lists of important issues to be resolved. When asked why there now appeared to be so little emphasis on a CTB, the representative of a major Middle Eastern NPT party replied that a CTB was nothing but a stick with which to beat the United States and, unlike the past, countries were beginning to realize that their own security was the most important issue. He went on to say that his country's concern was Israel's nuclear weapons, not a CTB.[9]

However, the CTB issue did become prominent during the 1990 NPT Review Conference. This was due primarily to the strong personal views of some representatives rather than commitment to the issue by governments. The Mexican representative, for example, personally was extremely committed to the notion of a CTB and demanded strongly worded language in the final document—language that was unacceptable to the United States. He refused to compromise, even though he could not muster support for his position from other countries.

The successful negotiation of the START treaty in 1991 and the follow-up announcements of even further arms cuts by the United States and Russia are very substantial accomplishments. The pace of arms control and disarmament activities by the two former Cold War adversaries has far exceeded those of the rest of the world. Nevertheless, non-nuclear-weapons states are likely to press for even further steps. In part, these states will be motivated by the belief that the much-reduced arsenals are still a great threat.

Other reasons that non-nuclear-weapons states are likely to keep up pressure regarding the disarmament issue include: It distracts attention from their own arms buildups; the superpower arms reductions do not include the arsenals of China, France, and the United Kingdom; and, momentum is supported by an "arms control bureaucracy" in Geneva, with a strong vested interest in continuing negotiations.

Security Assurances Following World War II, non-nuclear-weapons states were unsure whether and how the nuclear weapons states would use their arsenals. On one hand, there was the fact that nuclear weapons had been used against Japan to end the war, and on the other, a growing revulsion against the devastation these weapons caused. Non-nuclear-weapons states felt militarily threatened and were wary that nuclear weapons would be used to exert political pressure. During the negotiations on the NPT, the non-nuclear-weapons states sought assurances that the nuclear weapons states would not use or threaten to use their nuclear weapons against them and would help them if they were attacked by nuclear weapons.

To answer the need, the United States, United Kingdom, and Soviet Union agreed that positive security assurances should be given. In June 1968, they formalized their commitment in UN Security Council Resolution 255, which stated that "aggression with nuclear weapons against a non-nuclear-weapon state would create a situation in which the Security Council, and above all its nuclear-weapon-state permanent members, would have to act immediately in accordance with their obligations under the United Nations Charter."

Additionally, all five acknowledged nuclear weapons states individually have pledged a "negative security assurance," which is a promise not to attack, with nuclear weapons, any non-nuclear-weapons state party to the NPT. There are differences among the statements, however, and efforts to harmonize them have failed repeatedly. The Soviet statement excludes nations which allow nuclear weapons to be stationed on their soil. The US, UK, and French statements exclude those states that engage in an attack in alliance or association with a nuclear weapons state. These exceptions are based on the fact that the Soviet Union wished to include NATO states in its potential nuclear target set, and the Western allies sought to include Warsaw Pact nations in its set.

In NPT review conferences prior to 1990, the non-nuclear-weapons states criticized the positive and negative security assurances for their nonbinding nature and called for a legal commitment instead. In the preparations for the 1990 NPT Review Conference, however, scant attention was paid to the issue. This was despite the fact that the three depositary states—the United States, Soviet Union, and United Kingdom—worked in advance of the conference to find new language and mechanisms that would strengthen the assurances. The issue was raised at the review conference by Nigeria and Egypt, but no conclusion was reached for several reasons, including insufficient preparation and awareness of impending war with Iraq. The United States and United Kingdom were in no mood to enhance security assurances to NPT parties, of which Iraq was one.

In the future, the question of security assurances is likely to arise again. One reason is that there will inevitably be the question of how the United States intends to deter aggression by states with other weapons of mass destruction, namely chemical and biological. The United States has already forsworn possession or use of biological weapons and has pledged that it will not use chemical weapons, even if attacked with chemical weapons. Some national security specialists in the United States advocate that nuclear weapons are the appropriate threat to deter chemical or biological use, but many analysts disagree, saying that nuclear weapons would be an unacceptable alternative in any context other than vis-à-vis a nuclear threat.

Even if this is the decision of the United States, what about other nuclear weapons states? Israel, for example, implied that it would respond to an Iraqi chemical or biological attack with nuclear weapons. Would that also be the position of China, France, Russia, or the United Kingdom? Non-nuclear-weapons states might seek clarification by again stressing the issue of security assurances.

Absence of Punishment for Proliferators

If a nation chooses to acquire nuclear weapons—regardless of whether it is party to the NPT—it may do so with little fear of significant repercussions. There is no international consensus, within or outside of the treaty context, to take concerted action against a new nuclear weapons state. There are clear precedents—Israel, India, Pakistan—that demonstrate that a proliferator can anticipate angry words from the United States but not orchestrated military or economic actions.

The UN Special Commission established to identify and destroy Iraq's weapons of mass destruction is not likely to be a harbinger of what a proliferant can expect in the future. Action against Iraq is not punishment or reaction against its acts of proliferation per se. Rather, it is a part of the ceasefire resolutions which followed the Allied Coalition expulsion of Iraq from Kuwait. It is conceivable that there may be UN or international actions similar to those in Iraq against proliferators in the future. However, it is unlikely because such international consensus is very difficult to achieve. Had Iraq not undertaken such a blatant transgression, had the Cold War not just ended, and had Kuwait not been such a strategically important country, it is doubtful that the coalition which ousted Iraq from Kuwait would ever have been formed. Without that coalition and without the war, the UN Special Commission would not have been formed with the charter that it has to eliminate Iraqi nuclear weapons capabilities.

The fact that the NPT contains no provision for punishing proliferants does not foreclose the possibility that individual nations may strike others' nuclear programs. Israel's attack against Iraqi facilities that were associated with the latter's suspected nuclear weapons program is a case in point. The United States may undertake such strikes in the future, if its policy evolves from one of nonproliferation—seeking to prevent nations' proliferating—to one of counterproliferation. Counterproliferation implies a willingness to attack or sabotage a proliferant's program in the event that nonproliferation measures fail.

Attitudes of Nonaligned Parties

One weakness associated with the NPT is the prevailing attitude among less-developed countries of the nonaligned bloc that the treaty favors the advanced industrial states, particularly the treaty depositaries (United

States, United Kingdom, Russia). Rather than viewing the treaty as a means to their own security, nonaligned nations tend to portray the NPT as a tool of the "have nations" to keep the "have-nots" at a low level of technological development and political-military power so that they will not become threats.

One of the most frequently cited examples equating political power with nuclear weapons status is the fact that the five acknowledged nuclear weapons states are the only permanent members of the UN Security Council. In fact, however, the example is faulty. The five were first designated as permanent members of the Security Council. Only later did they develop nuclear weapons capabilities.

Gradually, an increasing number of non-nuclear-weapons states see the NPT as being in their own security interests. (Reasons why nonproliferation is in the security interests of non-nuclear-weapons states are detailed in Chapter 10.) They are also realizing that there are excellent examples of countries that have become exceedingly powerful economically and politically without nuclear weapons status. In fact, it can be argued that Japan and Germany have become as powerful as they have, in part, because they do not spend large sums on defense.

Performance of the NPT

Although many people expect the NPT to prevent nuclear proliferation, it cannot do so. Rather than evaluating the treaty on the basis of whether it actually prevents proliferation, it should be assessed in terms of its contribution to an environment that discourages countries' acquisition of nuclear weapons. In this regard, the treaty has very clear accomplishments.

Sets a Legal Barrier

The NPT is a legal document through which countries can make a political commitment not to proliferate. For those countries that respect international law, becoming party to the treaty means that they will obey its provisions.

In many, if not most, countries there is a strong commitment to any legal obligation undertaken. Any act of noncompliance is viewed as serious and will be carefully considered by the political leadership. If a decision is made to violate the treaty, the country in question is likely to want to hide its noncompliance. This will increase the financial cost of cheating because facilities will have to be hidden, emissions and other signatures masked, and secrecy maintained.

Although there are cases in which the legal obligations of the NPT have been ignored (e.g., Iraq and North Korea), the majority of nations party to the treaty have valued their legal obligations. It is impossible to say whether the treaty has actually stopped a nation from considering or undertaking a nuclear weapons program, but the existence of the treaty compels more careful consideration of such action. And, for treaty parties, it requires that they devote resources to trying to hide treaty noncompliance.

Creates a Norm

Since the first US nuclear test in 1945, attitudes toward nuclear proliferation have evolved. Whereas there was once a general political acceptance of the reality that any nation that wants nuclear weapons can have them, there is now a general sense that the spread of nuclear weapons is not acceptable because it threatens global political stability. The NPT has been central in establishing this negative view, this norm against proliferation.

Before the NPT entered into force, no document or set of principles existed around which a consensus against proliferation could coalesce. The treaty articulated the need to prevent proliferation.

Sets Apart the Suspect

Nations that refuse to become party to the NPT (or a regional nonproliferation treaty) identify themselves as potential proliferants. This is helpful to the nonproliferation regime in a few respects. It enables countries wishing to prevent the spread of nuclear weapons to focus their diplomatic pressures on the countries of greatest risk. It signals to the non-signatory's neighbors that they need to be wary and, perhaps, seek protection by means of security arrangements or their own military buildup. And, it allows supplier nations to selectively apply restrictions on exports of technology, equipment, and materials to the countries of greatest concern.

Establishes a Forum for Ongoing Dialog

A decision to pursue nuclear weapons can be—and historically has been—made by only a few people within a government. The decision is usually made without consultation and without benefit of public debate. Open discussion can be crucial in a government's decision not to proliferate, as is seen in the case of Sweden, a country that ended its weapons program after such a debate. (Chapter 10 sets out some of the arguments and points to be made in a dialog.)

The NPT provides a forum for public and government-to-government exchange on nonproliferation. Regular interactions between the depositary governments and other treaty parties, particularly in preparation for the review conferences of the treaty, are held every five years. A central topic in these interactions is a continuing reassessment of the value of the NPT and of the overall goal of nonproliferation.

Provides a Framework for Verification

Verification is a key to establishing trust among nations that no one of them is pursuing clandestine nuclear weapons capability. International safeguards are one means to provide some assurance that nuclear-related materials and facilities are not being used for weapons purposes.

While safeguards have not been wholly effective in detecting noncompliance (as in the case of Iraq), their deficiencies are caused primarily by technological and political limitations in the safeguards realm, not in treaty language. The safeguards regime could be strengthened, however, by NPT language that stressed the need to safeguard weaponization and undeclared nuclear activities. Despite this weakness, the NPT provides the basis for improving safeguards and their application. Without the treaty, development and application of safeguards would not be easy, and probably would not be as acceptable to the international community.

Conclusion

The NPT is a legal document by which nations can pledge not to further the spread of nuclear weapons. It is a voluntary commitment without mechanics for enforcement; there are no sanctions provided for violators.

The treaty is frought with problems ranging from insufficient membership to noncompliance and inadequate verifiability. Over time, the degree of concern over any given problem associated with the treaty has varied. For example, early preoccupation with nuclear-related assistance for peaceful programs has diminished somewhat with the decline in popularity of nuclear power.

Because the treaty cannot prevent proliferation and has many problems, some might conclude that it has not performed its mission well. If assessed on the basis of its contribution to creating obstacles against proliferation, however, the NPT has been very successful. It was central to the evolution of an international norm against the spread of nuclear weapons, posed a political barrier for treaty parties which might be contemplating proliferation, enabled a dialog on the pros and cons of proliferation, provided a mechanism for identifying those nations not committed to nonproliferation, and created the basis for safeguards and verification activities.

Notes

1. It is interesting that, thirty years later, the tables have turned. It is now the United States and NATO allies that are concerned about control over and nontransfer to third parties of Russian nuclear weapons stationed on the soil of the republics of Ukraine, Belarus, and Kazakhstan. Fears are that Russia may not have total physical control over the weapons.

2. For a discussion of these and other countries' nuclear weapons programs, see Leonard S. Spector with Jacqueline R. Smith, *Nuclear Ambitions* (Boulder, CO: Westview Press, 1990).

3. As is clear from the case of Iraq, it is possible for a nation's nuclear facilities to be hidden; there may be no evidence of a covert nuclear weapons program even when one exists.

4. George Lardner, Jr., and R. Jeffrey Smith, "Gates Warns of Iraqi Nuclear Aspirations," *The Washington Post*, December 16, 1992, p. A6.

5. The US decision to announce that it had no nuclear weapons remaining on South Korean soil was widely publicized in December 1991. For example, one report stated, "Supporting efforts by North and South Korea to resolve differences and move closer to unity, the United States has agreed to an unusual public statement that all bases in South Korea are nuclear free and that they could be open to inspection. The United States traditionally does not confirm or deny the presence of nuclear weapons or nuclear material." See Barbara Crossette, "US–North Korea Talks Planned on State of Nuclear Development," *The New York Times*, January 15, 1992, p. A12.

6. See Michael Breen, "North Korea's Nuclear Denials Set Stage for Challenge," *The Washington Times*, February 19, 1993, p. A1; R. Jeffrey Smith, "N. Korea Quitting Arms Pact," *The Washington Post*, March 12, 1993, p. A16; and Robert A. Manning and Leonard S. Spector, "North Korea's Nuclear Gambit," *The Washington Post*, March 21, 1993, p. C3.

7. Iraq's nuclear facilities were again bombed in 1991, this time by the allied coalition seeking to oust Saddam Hussein's armed forces from Kuwait. Public outcry over the bombing was muted not only by the multinational support of the coalition but also because of the later revelations of Iraq's violations of safeguards at the facilities.

8. There were other arms control agreements which addressed arms limitations and limits on nuclear testing—none of which were designed to *reduce* the numbers or types of weapons. Treaties banning biological and toxin weapons as well as chemical weapons use had been signed, but neither treaty was effectively verifiable, and the United States remained convinced that the Soviet Union was violating both.

9. This information is based on an official conversation between US government officials and those of a leading Middle Eastern nation. The author of this book was, at the time, responsible for US preparations for the NPT Review Conference and headed the discussions with foreign governments on the topic.

3

Supply-Side Policies: Why They Fail

The United States, the first nuclear weapons state, sought to keep secret the designs for its nuclear explosives as well as the means by which it created special nuclear materials (plutonium and enriched uranium) for its weapons. It did so by classifying weapons-related information and technologies (i.e., placing strict controls on disposition and dissemination) and limiting access to facilities. In other words, the first line of defense against proliferation of nuclear weapons was limiting the supply of knowledge and technologies.

Only four years after the first US nuclear test in 1945, the Soviet Union exploded its first nuclear device. Despite US efforts to keep its nuclear secrets, the USSR had acquired nuclear capabilities—partly through indigenous efforts, partly through espionage. Over the next two decades, proliferation by the United Kingdom, France, and China made it clear that nations with sufficient resources, will, and infrastructure could produce nuclear weapons. It was also clear that nations without significant financial and technical resources would be unable to develop such weaponry. This was because of the large-scale effort required, involving many technologies and construction of sophisticated, complex facilities. The single most costly and difficult step in the process was (and is) production of the fissile materials for nuclear explosives.

Drafters of the NPT realized the importance of controlling fissile materials as well as the equipment and processes to make them. They realized that the facilities, equipment, and materials that form the basis of a civil nuclear power industry could also be used to support a weapons program. In Article III, the NPT requires that parties to the treaty refrain from exporting key items—unless safeguards are applied—to non-nuclear-weapons states. The Article lists key items as:

- Source or special fissionable materials, and
- Equipment or material especially designed or prepared for the processing, use, or production of special fissionable material.

It should be noted that the NPT does not require specifically that the export of nuclear facilities trigger safeguards, even though it would seem logical that control of materials and equipment would imply control over facilities as well. David Fischer, a noted expert on the NPT and advisor to the IAEA, has noted that this left room for some countries to interpret the treaty as allowing export of a reprocessing or uranium enrichment facility without safeguards. "In fact, in the late 1970s Italy sold hot cells and a pilot fuel-fabrication plant to Iraq without letting the IAEA know or requiring safeguards."[1]

So that all parties to the NPT could agree on exactly what exports would need safeguards, the Zangger Committee was formed.[2] "The Zangger Committee ... produced and keeps up-to-date a list of material and equipment 'especially designed or prepared' for nuclear use as well as definitions of technology, major critical components and the criteria needed to interpret the trigger list."[3]

Even though the NPT requires safeguards on key items and the Zangger Committee detailed exactly what those items are, there could be no guarantee that a nation would not use foreign-supplied technology to make nuclear weapons despite safeguards or assurances. For example, India built its own unsafeguarded reactor based on knowledge gained from a safeguarded reactor from Canada. India tested a nuclear explosive in 1974.

Nuclear-supplier states—the nations with the capability to export equipment and materials for civil nuclear programs—responded to India's test by further tightening export controls. They formed the Nuclear Suppliers Group, also referred to as the London Club. One of the most important respects in which it differed from the Zangger Committee was that it included France, a nonparty to the NPT.

The Nuclear Suppliers Group placed safeguards not only on export of nuclear materials and equipment, but on sensitive nuclear technologies (i.e., enrichment, reprocessing, and heavy-water production). Also, the club used the Zangger Committee list and added to it. In the late 1970s and throughout the 1980s, there were repeated efforts to strengthen and lengthen the list of controlled items, but agreement within the club was not reached. In 1992, following the revelations regarding the Iraqi weapons programs, consensus was finally reached on adding some dual-use items (items that can be used for other purposes than just nuclear-related functions). Additionally, European nuclear suppliers (including Russia[4]) adopted a policy already being implemented by the United States: full-scope safeguards. This means that they will not supply nuclear equipment, technology, or materials to any non-nuclear-weapons state that does not subject the entirety of its nuclear program to safeguards.

Despite lengthening the list of items controlled and tightening the application of controls through licensing and oversight, nuclear export

controls—and supply-side policies in general—do not stop nuclear proliferation. Their greatest value is and has been to slow programs, during
which time diplomatic and other pressures may work to deter the country
in question from pursuing nuclear weapons. The principal problems with
supply-side policies are outlined below.

Membership

Suppliers' groups have a problem similar to that of the NPT: Key
countries may decline to participate, or they may not be invited to join.
Several countries not in the Nuclear Suppliers Group are now capable of
exporting nuclear materials, equipment, or technology that could assist a
proliferant's nuclear weapons program. Brazil, China, India, and some
states devolved from the former Soviet Union are "second-tier suppliers"
able to export nuclear items, unconstrained by the Nuclear Suppliers Group
or a policy of full-scope safeguards.

Iranian attempts to import nuclear technology demonstrate the problem
of second-tier suppliers. Even though Iran is a signatory of the NPT and
would likely place its nuclear exports under safeguards, there have been
fears—particularly by the United States and United Kingdom—that Iran
would be willing to break safeguards and not comply with the NPT in its
efforts to acquire nuclear weapons capability. They and other nations
participating in the Nuclear Suppliers Group agreed to treat Iran as a
country of concern and to refrain from nuclear exports there. However,
second-tier suppliers were ready to provide the nuclear supplies that group
members were unwilling to sell to Iran.

In June 1990, Iran signed a contract with China to purchase a 20-
megawatt research reactor and some small-scale calutron equipment.[5]
News of this agreement became public knowledge following revelations in
1991 that Iraq had used calutrons—a relatively inefficient and dated technology—to enrich uranium for its nuclear weapons program. Concerns
were expressed by governments and in the media regarding the Chinese-
supplied technology, and there were reports that China would not proceed
with the export of a research reactor.[6] Iran tried to defuse the situation by
declaring its peaceful intentions and inviting a special visit by the International Atomic Energy Agency, an offer that was accepted. The visit in
February 1992 revealed no surprises and public concerns about Iran
somewhat diminished.[7] Easing of suspicions may have cleared the way for
the export of the Chinese research reactor to Iran. In early 1993, the director
of Iran's Atomic Energy Commission said that the sale would go forward.[8]

China was not the only second-tier country from which Iran was seeking
nuclear assistance. In 1991, India negotiated a contract to provide Iran with
a 10-megawatt reactor[9] and held discussions on selling it a 220-megawatt

power reactor.[10]   Although India stated that the facility would be under safeguards, the United States and others put intense pressure on India to not make the sale. An Indian official tried to deflect the pressures, saying, "Our offer to Iran is exactly like the nuclear reactors set up by Argentina in Algeria and Peru."[11] India ultimately decided against the export.

Argentina was another supplier-country considering nuclear sales to Iran. Iran held talks with Argentina to supply fuel-fabrication equipment and other technology.[12] Only after the United States agreed to help compensate Argentina for the loss of the sale did Argentina decline the export.[13] For Argentina to have made the sale would not have been unprecedented; it had already sold small nuclear research reactors to Peru and Algeria. Argentina decided not to continue supplying technology to potential proliferants and joined the Nuclear Suppliers Group in December 1992. One of its incentives for doing so was to increase the flow of high technology from industrialized states which otherwise would have treated Argentina as a country of concern and itself a potential proliferation risk.

"Haves" Versus "Have-Nots"

The nuclear nonproliferation regime has been plagued with a rift between those countries which possess nuclear technologies and those that do not. Many countries in the latter group deeply resent what they view as efforts to deny them technology. They say that export controls are actually motivated by a desire to keep them underdeveloped. Their argument is that if technologies related to nuclear weapons or fissile materials production should be forsworn by less-developed states, then they should also be given up by the advanced-industrial states as well. If that is not possible or desirable, then any country that commits itself to peaceful uses of nuclear technologies should have access to those technologies.

The prevailing view among states in the Nuclear Suppliers Group is that political commitments to peaceful uses of nuclear technologies are insufficient; they can act as a smoke screen behind which nations can pursue nuclear weapons. Thus, in the interests of nonproliferation, nuclear technologies should not be widely shared and, in the event they are exported, should be safeguarded.

These decisions by the Zangger Committee and, to a much greater extent, the Nuclear Suppliers Group have promoted the perception that technology denial is adversarial. Both groups have limited membership, and the Nuclear Suppliers Group primarily comprises advanced nuclear technology suppliers. For reasons associated with the domestic politics in France at the time, the Nuclear Suppliers Group met in secret from the outset. "This enhanced the impression that it was a secret cartel of First and Second World suppliers ganging up on the Third World."[14]

The gap between the "haves" and "have-nots" cannot be bridged easily. Many new supplier nations in the second tier are reluctant to join the category of "haves" because they would then be in the position they themselves have reviled: the position of exercising prejudice against the "have nots," the group of which they were formerly a member. If they do join the Nuclear Suppliers Group, as Argentina did, they may do so with the expectation of financial or technological reward, such as increased high-technology imports.

Even if new-supplier states are willing to join in the Nuclear Suppliers Group, there may be a risk that they will work to weaken rather than strengthen export controls. For example, they may argue that the lists of equipment subject to export controls should be kept static, or even shortened. They may also oppose more stringent application of licensing procedures or expenditure of resources to train and develop nations' export-control bureaucracies.

A more important problem with widening the membership of the Nuclear Suppliers Group is the possibility that the very targets of the export controls—countries which are high proliferation risks—will become members in order to obtain the benefits of membership. A principal benefit is easier access to high technology. Because membership in an export controls group is increasingly seen by the United States and some other nations as a symbol of a "responsible" nonproliferation policy, they tend to loosen the export controls exercised toward members of the group. Just as Iraq used membership in the NPT as a smoke screen for its true intentions, countries may use membership in a suppliers group to hide their own proliferation aspirations.

Circumvention

Several nations—including Pakistan, Iraq, and Israel—have proven the ease with which export controls can be circumvented. A variety of techniques have been used. At times, countries or, more usually, companies willingly participate in subterfuge. Other times, the exporting firm may be duped. False bills-of-lading, shipment through multiple countries, or use of front companies enable the importing nation to evade controls.

Some importing nations acquire subcomponents or raw materials rather than the end product which is controlled. For example, Iraq had difficulty in acquiring equipment crafted from maraging steel. So, it imported the maraging steel instead, with the intention of fabricating within Iraq the requisite parts.

In the future, it may become easier for nefarious companies in Europe to collude with proliferant nations, particularly in the case of dual-use goods. At the end of 1992, the European Economic Community will end restrictions on intra-Community trade in dual-use goods. It will be relatively simple to export controlled items via other countries. For example, a German company may acknowledge that sale of a particular component is limited by Nuclear Suppliers Group controls. Nevertheless, it may export that item to Greece or some other European Community (EC) nation, which is not illegal. From there, the component could be reexported more easily because Greece and certain other EC members do not have substantial resources dedicated to export controls. Although it would still be illegal for the German company to export the item to Greece knowing that it would be reexported, it would be very hard to prove that the German company was at fault if it denied any knowledge of the reexport plans. The EC is aware of the problem and has tried to devise a common approach to export controls. The success of these measures will depend largely on progress in the European political and economic union.

Indigenous Production

One of the most serious challenges to supply-side nonproliferation policies is the growth of indigenous technical capabilities in proliferant nations. Once nations can produce equipment and facilities for themselves, export controls by supplier nations become irrelevant.

Proliferant nations may succeed in mastering highly complex technologies using native personnel and relatively few imports. Pakistan's uranium enrichment program is such a case. Pakistani nationals returned to their native country after working abroad with high technology. In some cases they brought only their skills and experience. In the case of uranium centrifuge-enrichment technology, however, design plans and equipment lists were stolen. These became the basis of Pakistan's successful indigenous production capability.

Iraq is another example of successful indigenous capabilities. By choosing a relatively easier method of uranium enrichment—electro-magnetic isotope separation—Iraq was able to tackle a technology it could master. As a result, Iraq was able to produce, by itself, major components, including the giant magnets used in the uranium-isotope separation machines.

Indigenous production is often dependent on some imports of raw materials and nonsensitive, noncontrollable commodities. Iraq imported the large magnet-iron blanks from which it machined magnet pole pieces, for example. Such items, however, are used very widely in industry and can be obtained from such a variety of sources that it would be impossible to control them.

Dual-Use Equipment

The effectiveness of export controls is also diluted by the availability and use of dual-use equipment (e.g., items also used in legitimate non-weapons-related functions). Again, Iraq provides an example. Iraq imported large quantities of machinery and materials that are commonly used for civil purposes. Whenever questioned regarding their end-use, Iraq gave logical explanations of how the imports would be used in non-weapons-related projects. For example, Iraq needed power-supply equipment for its uranium-enrichment plant. Baghdad imported these items, saying they were for other industrial power-supply purposes.[15]

Increasingly, efforts are being made—particularly by the United States—to control dual-use technologies and equipment. Some progress has been made in obtaining participation of others in controls on dual-use items. The twenty-four nations of the Nuclear Suppliers Group have agreed to add 65 dual-use items to their control lists. However, the list will be difficult to extend further, and the existing list will be hard to enforce. As Paul Leventhal has noted, "Further refining the list of dual-use items can become a technological and political swamp, judging by past difficulties encountered in the interagency deliberations in the US government alone. Better to concentrate on upgrading national and international controls on *nuclear* items whose significance for weapons is not debatable but which nonetheless remain uncontrolled or inadequately controlled."[16]

One reason for problems with dual-use controls is lack of consensus on the need or propriety of controlling dual-use items. It can be convincingly argued that preventing free trade in dual-use equipment and technologies is detrimental to the economic and social development of less-developed countries. The United States may make the argument that a country like Iran should be deprived of dual-use items because it is "guilty of proliferation until proven innocent," despite Iran's claim that it is not pursuing nuclear weapons. Other exporting nations, however, are not as convinced that Iran is up to no good. They say that unless it can be proven that Iran has a nuclear weapons program—or at a minimum that it leaves the NPT and breaks its safeguards obligations—it should be eligible to import machine tools and other equipment, even if they could be applied to a weapons program.

A second reason that controls on dual-use equipment are likely to fail is the widespread availability of such equipment. Because most dual-use items are usable in multiple industries and functions, they tend to be manufactured by many companies and countries. In fact, the availability of such equipment may even be increased as a result of the items' inclusion on export-control lists. This is because new suppliers, seeing the opportunity to meet a demand where supply has diminished, may seek to fill the gap.[17]

A third reason is ease of manufacture or substitute. Even though proliferant nations often try to import dual-use equipment, often they do so for convenience and to save time. In many cases, the dual-use items imported could be manufactured indigenously, if a concerted effort were made to do so. In other cases, substitutes will suffice. For example, computers sold over-the-counter can be upgraded with performance accelerators, making them an adequate substitute for high-performance computers now subject to export controls.

Motivation

The single greatest shortcoming of supply-side policies is their failure to address the motivations underlying proliferation. Generally, nations are motivated to acquire nuclear weapons because they seek additional security vis-à-vis a perceived enemy, desire the prestige associated with advanced weaponry, and/or wish to engage in aggression. None of these is diminished by controls over nuclear technology.

It is conceivable that supply-side policies may indirectly promote proliferation. As the availability of items on the Nuclear Suppliers Group list shrinks, the prices consumers are willing to pay may rise. If so, new suppliers may enter the market, expecting to reap high profits. Thus, the incentives listed above may be joined by a relatively new one—financial. Having nuclear-related technology could become a way to earn hard currency. Although there is no evidence that this has happened in the arena of nuclear proliferation, it has occurred in the case of missile proliferation. North Korea, for example, is reaping hard currency profits by selling the types of missiles now restricted under missile export controls.

Yet another motivation for acquiring nuclear weapons in the future may be for political blackmail. Some republics of the former Soviet Union have used the issue of nuclear weapons possession to try to wrest political and financial concessions from Western countries. (This is discussed in greater detail in Chapter 4.) Similarly, North Korea has manipulated Western countries interested in assuring a nuclear-weapons-free Korean Peninsula. Pyongyang used the threat of a North Korean weapons program to force the United States to assure that it has no nuclear weapons based in South Korea and to downgrade exercises between US and South Korean troops. Will nations in the future be motivated to acquire nuclear weapons so that they can use them for political benefit?

Conclusion

Supply-side policies should not be abandoned. Classification of technical information as well as export controls both play a constructive role in delaying nations' efforts to acquire nuclear weapons. This time delay can be crucial, enabling an opportunity to rethink the pros and cons of nuclear weapons possession. The delay can also give other nations a chance to try to influence the potential proliferant by providing security measures, diplomatic pressures, or other incentives and disincentives.

Efforts to tweak supply-side policies, or to make them the central focus of nuclear nonproliferation measures, are unlikely to be worth the resources they will require. Not only are they unlikely to be effective, they may actually distract valuable energies and resources from nonproliferation policies that could be more constructive.

Notes

1. David Fischer, "The London Club and the Zangger Committee: How Effective?," in Bailey and Rudney, Eds., *Proliferation and Export Controls* (New York: University Press of America, 1993), p. 42.

2. The committee was named after Claude Zangger, a Swiss expert who chaired it.

3. Fischer, op. cit., p. 40.

4. Russia did not apply its requirement for full-scope safeguards to recently completed nuclear contracts, one of which was with India for nuclear power reactors.

5. R. Jeffrey Smith, "Officials Say Iran Is Seeking Nuclear Weapons Capability," *The Washington Post*, October 30, 1991, p. 1.

6. Steve Coll, "US Halted Nuclear Bid By Iran," *The Washington Post*, November 17, 1992, p. 1.

7. Michael Z. Wise, "Atom Team Reports on Iran Probe," *The Washington Post*, February 15, 1992, p. 29.

8. Claude von England, "Iran Defends Its Pursuit of Nuclear Technology," *Christian Science Monitor*, February 18, 1993, p. 7.

9. This reactor would not produce very much weapons-grade material. It would need to be run 24 hours a day for a year to produce enough plutonium for one device.

10. Steve Coll, "Iran Reported Trying to Buy Indian Reactor," *The Washington Post*, November 15, 1991, p. 33.

11. Statement by P.K. Iyengar, chairman of the Indian Atomic Energy Commission, carried by DPA news service November 20, 1991.

12. One estimate stated that the deal was worth over $18 million to Argentina. Michael Z. Wise, op. cit.

13. In March 1992, Investigaciones Aplicadas signed a memorandum of understanding to develop future business with General Atomics, Inc., with the support of the US government, to help Argentina make up for the loss of the sale to Iran. See Steve Coll, "US Halted Nuclear Bid By Iran," *The Washington Post*, November 17, 1992, pp. 1, A30.

14. Fischer, op. cit., p. 40.

15. See "Iraqi Circumvention of Export Controls" in Kathleen C. Bailey, et al., *Iraq Inspections: Lessons Learned*, US Defense Nuclear Agency Report No. DNA-TR-92-115, January, 1993.

16. Paul Leventhal, "Nuclear Export Controls: Can We Plug the Leaks?" in Jean-Francois Rioux (editor), *Limiting the Proliferation of Weapons: The Role of Supply-Side Strategies* (Ottawa: Carleton University Press, 1992), p. 47.

17. This phenomenon has already occurred in the case of other export–control regimes. For example, India became a supplier of a key chemical usable in chemical weapons when the Australia Group, a suppliers group similar to the Nuclear Suppliers Group, placed export controls on it. And, North Korea and others have begun to export ballistic missiles and components in the face of tight controls by suppliers who are member to the Missile Technology Control Regime.

4

Limitations of Detection
and Verification

Detection and verification provide deterrence as well as reassurance to participants in the nuclear nonproliferation regime. A potential cheater may be deterred from acquiring nuclear weapons because the threat of being caught is too great. At the same time, a nation that does not want to cheat will be reassured that others are in compliance with nonproliferation agreements if it has confidence that cheating can be detected.

There are two keys to the success of detection and verification. The first is technology. Technical tools must exist to detect, for example, illicit nuclear production reactors and reprocessing activities. Equally important, there must be the political will and ability to apply those technical tools in a rigorous manner. Having the ability to detect clandestine uranium enrichment is pointless if the suspect country will not allow use of the tools or if the user of the tools is lax.

In the case of the nuclear nonproliferation regime and, in particular, safeguards, there have been serious deficiencies in detection and verification, most clearly in the case of Iraq. Western governments and the International Atomic Energy Agency (IAEA) were unaware of the extent of Iraq's clandestine nuclear activities. This example convinces many nations that they can no longer trust the detection and verification capabilities and procedures currently used by the IAEA to uncover secret weapons programs. Furthermore, they cannot have confidence that Western governments will have foreknowledge of clandestine nuclear programs and the willingness to act on the basis of that information. This problem is doubly serious because the absence of effective detection tools may free potential proliferants from worry of being caught and increase the likelihood that they will undertake nuclear weapons programs.

There must be improvements in the detection and verification capabilities and procedures associated with nuclear nonproliferation to restore nations' confidence that cheating can and will be discovered. To better understand this challenge, it is useful to review the Iraqi nuclear weapons program and its implications for the nuclear nonproliferation regime. This chapter will focus on the limitations of the verification regime; Chapter 7 will explore alternatives for improving verification.

Iraq's Nuclear Weapons Program[1]

In 1969, Iraq ratified the Nuclear Nonproliferation Treaty (NPT) and later, in 1972, signed a safeguards agreement with the IAEA. Despite its declared commitment to nuclear nonproliferation, Iraq was suspected of working to establish nuclear weapons capability. In 1976, it purchased from France a large (40 megawatt) research reactor capable of producing significant quantities of plutonium and, from Italy, three hot cells in which small quantities of plutonium could be separated from irradiated fuel. Iraq also began to negotiate for a large heavy-water power reactor (that could have produced large amounts of plutonium) and a reprocessing facility.

In 1980, Iraq undertook two actions that suggested its intent to produce plutonium. It purchased large amounts of natural uranium on the open market—material which could not be used as fuel for its research reactor because it required highly enriched uranium. The natural uranium would, however, be useful for a heavy-water power reactor. Second, Iraq contracted with a West German firm, NUKEM, to purchase depleted-uranium-metal fuel pins that could be irradiated in the research reactor to produce plutonium.

Israel, convinced that Iraq was seeking nuclear weapons capability, bombed the French-supplied Osiraq research reactor in June 1981, shortly before the reactor was due to start up. This attack set the Iraqi program back but did not stop it. Iraq renewed its efforts, concentrating greater attention on concealment. Baghdad developed an elaborate plan of camouflage, concealment, and deception to assure secrecy for its nuclear weapons development program. It also sought to increase the chances of success by diversifying the technologies used in the nuclear weapons program.

Iraq pursued both enrichment of uranium and separation of plutonium. Initially, four different methods of uranium enrichment were attempted: gaseous diffusion, electromagnetic isotope separation (EMIS), gas centrifuge, and chemical enrichment. Diffusion reportedly was dropped in the late 1980s because it was too complicated and risky. Substantial progress had been made on the other three, especially EMIS and gas centrifuge, at the time Desert Storm began in January 1991.

Baghdad also emphasized indigenous production of components and materials. This helped make Iraq independent of suppliers and prevent discovery of its program by Western intelligence agencies that monitor global import–export markets. When it was not possible to produce an item indigenously, Iraq would attempt to purchase subcomponents or precursors and assemble them domestically. To further confuse any potential observers of its EMIS program, Iraq diversified the sources from which it acquired subcomponents. As former IAEA inspector David Kay noted, the

Iraqis had "...a very high level of project management. That is, they could order one piece of equipment from the United States; match it with software or measuring equipment from another country; and integrate a third piece of equipment when the package arrived in Iraq. So, literally, no single manufacturer really knew what the equipment was being used for or would be used for in Iraq."[2]

When Iraq could not make or assemble the needed items itself, it acquired them abroad, often in large quantities for contingency stockpiles. Iraq tried to use dual-use equipment and materials whenever possible. Imports were made through surreptitious means, often involving front companies, trans-shipment through multiple countries, and false bills-of-lading. To some extent, Iraq sought out and gained cooperation from unscrupulous companies. However, it ordinarily did not trust the companies and attempted to keep them in the dark about the uses for the imports. For example, Iraq would claim that an item was needed for a civilian entity such as the Ministry of Health. Because the cited end-use was usually legitimate and logical, the exporting company would have no reason to doubt the Iraqi claim.

To improve its indigenous technical capabilities, Iraq solicited bids for technology transfer but never allowed the process to materialize into a contract. Foreign firms would bid for the job and transfer significant technical data in attempts to entice Iraq to give them the contract. When Iraq had gotten all that it thought possible from the process, it would cut off the negotiations. In some cases, Iraq may have gotten all of the information it needed to do the job itself. An example of this technique is Iraqi solicitation for building an underground nuclear reactor. Between 1982 and 1986, Iraq held discussions with the Soviet Union, a French–Belgian consortium, and China. After obtaining plans, answers to questions, and a variety of technical information, Iraq ended the negotiations, saying the project was too expensive. This incident has led some UN Special Commission (UNSCOM) inspectors to believe that Iraq may have a hidden plutonium-production reactor, perhaps located underground.

Iraq gave great attention to assuring secrecy of its program. Personnel were strictly controlled and individuals divulged information only at risk of their lives. Physical characteristics of facilities were altered to minimize the potential for raising suspicions. For example, power lines for the EMIS facility were run underground well away from the building to avoid drawing attention to the tremendous amount of energy being used at the site. Every effort was made to secure communications so that foreign intelligence-gathering could not learn of the program through eavesdropping. Detectable emissions from buildings were minimized. Misleading code names were given to the nuclear activities (e.g., the nuclear weapons program was called "Petrochemical Project-3").

NPT and IAEA safeguards were also a part of the deception plan. As a party to the NPT, Iraq was able to argue—successfully to many audiences—that it supported international nuclear nonproliferation goals. Iraq capitalized on the belief by some people that no country would go to the trouble of signing and ratifying an international arms control agreement and then violate it.

The Iraqi deception plan worked. US intelligence analyses correctly identified that Iraq was undertaking highly suspicious activities and might have a nuclear weapons program. But, there was no conclusive, irrefutable evidence, and nothing was known about the Iraqi secret uranium-enrichment facilities. Thus, when President Bush stated that the coalition in Desert Storm was determined to knock out Saddam Hussein's nuclear bomb potential, he was derided by some arms control analysts.

One article confidently claimed that "Iraq's nuclear weapons research and related activities are almost certainly carried out at only a few sites, and the major ones are largely devoted to other activities" and that "...the nuclear effort was at such an early stage that there was little to destroy."[3] Nobody recognized that Iraq might have hidden facilities. Another article claimed that the Bush administration was hyping the notion of an Iraqi bomb just to increase support for going to war against Saddam Hussein and concluded that Iraq was five to ten years away from having a nuclear weapon,[4] a point later disproven by UN inspections.

In fact, Iraq could have produced enough highly enriched uranium for a weapon in 18 months, had Desert Storm not begun. If Iraqi attempts to upgrade its facilities or the enrichment level of its uranium feedstocks had been successful, the time could have been further reduced.[5]

The United Nations Inspections

Following Desert Storm, UN Security Council Resolution 687 (UNSCR 687) required that the IAEA, in conjunction with the UN Special Commission (UNSCOM) on Iraq, inspect Iraqi nuclear sites and destroy equipment and facilities related to the nuclear weapons program. (UNSCR 687 similarly addresses other weapons of mass destruction and missile delivery systems.) To this end, UNSCR 687 ordered Iraq to declare all of its relevant weapons, materials, equipment, and facilities. It also ordered Iraq to facilitate the inspections and destructions processes. However, while maintaining a facade of cooperation, Iraq obstructed the process and attempted to defeat the purposes of UNSCR 687.

Iraq did not comply with UNSCR 687 from the outset. It did not declare its nuclear weapons program. Instead, it declared only the Tuwaitha site and the materials already under safeguards. As inspectors uncovered elements of the nuclear program, Iraq would usually admit them but not volunteer additional data. A report by IAEA Director General Hans Blix, dated January 20, 1992, summarizes Iraqi behavior:

> *The response of Iraq to the inspection work of the IAEA has largely followed a pattern of denial of clandestine activities until the evidence is overwhelming, followed by cooperation until the next case of concealment is revealed. As a consequence of this behavior, it is not possible to be confident that the full extent of prohibited nuclear activities has been disclosed. Continuation of the inspected activities, in parallel with the monitoring program, is deemed necessary.*[6]

Iraq sought to deprive the UN inspectors of information in other ways too. Even before the first nuclear inspection, Iraq removed or destroyed information and documentation that would have revealed its program. The first team reported:

> *The team was particularly concerned by the fact that many Iraqi statements were not supported by any source documentation—production records of the fuel fabrication plant, nuclear material transfer records, reactor operation records, fuel history cards, etc. The Iraqi authorities claimed that these documents/records had been destroyed, but in the light of various observations (e.g., of empty but unburnt filing cabinets) the team does not consider this to be a credible explanation; moreover, one would have expected that, with a functioning national nuclear materials accounting system, the Iraqis would have kept duplicates of relevant documents at the IAEC's [Iraqi Atomic Energy Agency's] establishments.*[7]

Iraq tried to prevent UN and IAEA inspectors from visiting sites that were part of its secret nuclear program. Baghdad asserted that only those facilities and materials already declared and under safeguards could be inspected.[8] UNSCOM firmly disagreed. Iraq enforced its view during the second nuclear-team visit (UNSCOM 4/IAEA 2)[9] by denying right of access to two sites that the inspectors wanted to visit. Furthermore, the Iraqis contravened inspectors' orders by removing equipment and materials related to uranium enrichment.

The problems with Iraqi noncompliance led to the passage of yet another UN Security Council Resolution, 707, on August 15, 1991. It condemned Iraq's behavior, demanded complete disclosure of its weapons programs, and required that Iraq facilitate the inspections. Two months later, another Security Council Resolution, 715, was passed to insist once again on Iraqi cooperation. (See Appendix A for texts of resolutions.) Nevertheless, problems persisted.

Despite Iraq's noncooperation, the first two UN/IAEA inspections were successful in some regards. They uncovered the fact that Iraq had separated plutonium in violation of safeguards[10] and had major uranium-enrichment facilities that had not been declared. Iraq continued to stonewall; it admitted the existence of the enrichment facilities, but offered alternative explanations for them. For example, it said that the second EMIS facility at Ash Sharqat was for plastic coating of equipment, which was nonsense.

Some of the Iraqi "cover stories" made sense, even though they were untrue. For example, two Japanese-manufactured streak video cameras, useful in weaponization tests, were found. Iraqis claimed that they were for graduate student work on internal combustion engines at the Technical University of Baghdad. This claim could not be disproven.

During the fourth nuclear inspection, it became clear to inspectors and UNSCOM that Iraq was making every effort to prevent discovery and destruction of the full scope of its nuclear program. Iraqis told inspectors that they had been hiding previously undeclared fuel elements that had been irradiated in violation of safeguards. To prevent their discovery during earlier inspections, Iraq placed the fuel on a truck and moved it around the Tuwaitha site as inspectors moved to other locations within the same site. Also, large amounts of equipment and documentation were removed. In reply to inspectors' requests for access to the equipment, Iraqi officials said that it was being used elsewhere in Iraq for peaceful purposes, a strategy they were to use repeatedly to prevent destruction.

When Iraq did provide information, it would not provide it in a timely way and often would often try to use delivery to disadvantage inspectors. In some cases, Iraq would deliver the data on the last day of an inspection. The team would be unable to act on the information without extending their stay. Iraq had quickly learned that UNSCOM was loathe to extend the stay of any team for a variety of reasons, including expense. There were many examples of this tactic, including one when Iraq released information about high explosives usable in nuclear weapons. The fourth nuclear inspection team had sought information on Iraqi imports of the explosive HMX. Iraq did not reveal that it had purchased hundreds of metric tons of HMX until the last day of the inspection, when the team had little time to act on the revelation.

On other occasions, Iraq would hold information and deliver it at the outset of an inspection. Iraq would provide data on the first day, overwhelming the team with new information. Also, Iraqis would sometimes deliver answers to questions in Arabic, when it would have been quite easy for them to do so in English. This delayed the inspection teams, while they awaited translation.

At times, Iraq would physically prevent inspectors from acquiring data. For example, a defector had given the location of documentation for the Iraqi nuclear weapons design effort to the sixth nuclear inspection team. This information enabled the team to seize sensitive documents that were very revealing. As inspectors departed, Iraqi officials stopped them and confiscated the documents. Iraq later returned many of the documents but withheld the most sensitive ones.

There were also instances in which Iraq destroyed an entire facility to deprive inspectors of information on its function and previous contents. Prior to the first nuclear team's visit, Iraq removed an extensive reinforced-concrete floor from the Nuclear Physics Laboratory at Tuwaitha. By the time of the second inspection, the building had been leveled and the site cleared.[11] Other efforts to deceive inspectors included painting walls to hamper sampling for presence of uranium; tearing out electrical grids to impede estimates of power usage; and covering over transport rails with concrete to hide them.

The inspectors dealt consistently with the same group of Iraqis—presumably to minimize the potential for accidental leaks of information. Following the second nuclear inspection, when inspectors used videotaping and cameras, the Iraqis began videotaping inspections and continued the practice for all inspections. Inspectors felt that this Iraqi action provided teaching tools to help Iraqis better handle inspectors, intimidated their own people about revealing too much information, documented and exploited inspectors' "misbehavior," intimidated inspectors, and established "video parity" with inspectors.

When inspectors persisted, Iraqis occasionally responded with threat of force. Warning shots were fired on one occasion when three inspectors did not obey restrictions. And, Iraqis sometimes refused to guarantee safe passage of UN helicopters.

At times, intimidation of inspectors was "unofficial." Anonymous notes threatening to kill people were slipped under inspectors' hotel-room doors on at least one occasion.[12] UN personnel in Baghdad were splattered with paint, insulted in restaurants, and had clothing in their hotel rooms doused with acid.[13] Some inspectors have said the tension generated by these events was extremely wearing and that it impinged on the abilities of people on the team to do their jobs.

To some extent, the limitations on UN inspectors were self-imposed rather than applied by the Iraqis. IAEA inspectors argued repeatedly that a nonconfrontational attitude must be maintained toward Iraq because the IAEA needed to have a long-term relationship with Iraq. If inspections were anything but cordial and nonaggressive, the Iraqis could make life very difficult for subsequent inspections or, even worse, unilaterally withdraw from safeguards. Also, IAEA representatives worried that confrontational inspections would deter other countries (such as North Korea, which was then considering whether to conclude a safeguards agreement) from participating in the safeguards program.

Iraq's intransigence and hostile attitude did affect the inspections. In July 1992, Iraq declared that the UN could not inspect its Ministry of Agriculture building. The dispute dragged on for over three weeks. Unconfirmed intelligence reports have stated that Iraq succeeded in removing evidence during this time.[14] When the inspection finally took place, nothing incriminating was found. Furthermore, Iraq succeeded in dictating terms of the inspection when it did take place. At Baghdad's insistence, the team did not include representatives from any country that had attacked Iraq during Desert Storm. Further evidence of Iraq's influence over the inspections process became clear a few weeks later, in August, when UNSCOM canceled a planned inspection of a military ministry declared off-limits by Iraq.[15]

Lessons for the Nonproliferation Regime

The key conclusion drawn from the Iraqi case is that the nuclear nonproliferation regime cannot prevent a determined proliferant, even when that nation is a participant in the regime. Iraq was a party to the NPT and placed its declared facilities under safeguards. Previously, it was widely acknowledged that the regime could not prevent proliferation in countries that refused to participate in nonproliferation measures such as the NPT. Yet, it was also widely assumed that a participant in the regime would be deterred and inhibited from seeking nuclear weapons capability by the regime's restraints and safeguards measures. Iraq proved that the regime can be readily circumvented and can be used as a smoke screen to obscure its nuclear weapon activities.

A second lesson from the Iraq case is that the traditional measures used to detect illicit activities and verify compliance with nonproliferation commitments are inadequate. Despite its routine inspections in Iraq, the IAEA was unaware that Iraq had reprocessed very small quantities of plutonium,[16] built undeclared facilities for uranium enrichment, or established a weapons program. If the IAEA had had some knowledge of the Iraqi weapons program, it could have tried to use its right to conduct special inspections to examine suspect sites. But even Western intelligence-collection efforts had failed to detect the extent and nature of the program.

A third lesson from the Iraq case is that equipment and facilities may be destroyed, but the basis for a nuclear weapons program may survive. Even when a program is uncovered and noncompliance declared, there is little that can be done to prevent proliferation in the long run if the country in question is determined to acquire nuclear weapons. Despite the extensive destruction of its facilities and equipment by UNSCOM and IAEA inspectors, Iraq technically can rebuild its weapons program, as it did after Israel's bombing of Osiraq, if it is motivated to do so. If IAEA and UNSCOM efforts to destroy and monitor Iraqi capabilities flag—whether because of lack of interest or mounting costs—Iraq can reinitiate the program. Iraq retains the basic building blocks for a renewed program, including:

- Key personnel;
- Documentation, plans, records, and design information; and,
- Large quantities of equipment removed from nuclear sites.

As CIA Director James Woolsey has said, "Iraq retains key nonfissile materials and equipment, such as centrifuge drawings, machine tools, and expertise, that it could use to rebuild a centrifuge-based uranium-enrichment effort."[17] Regarding Iraq's ability to restart its nuclear weapons program, the head of an UNSCOM nuclear inspection team, Dimitri Perricos, said, "The brains are there. They have good engineers. They have the machine tools to be able to start things again."[18]

Potentially, there are undiscovered facilities as well. There may be a centrifuge facility or, as mentioned above, a hidden production reactor. Also, Iraq may still possess materials it has said were destroyed by bombing. For example, it declared that over two tons of heavy water were lost in the war, but there is no proof of this. Approximately ten times this amount would be needed for a research reactor, but the point is that there may be many things hidden which, when pulled together, form the basis for a renewed program.

The means currently used by Western governments to detect nuclear proliferation activities are inadequate, as are the techniques and practices of the IAEA. The case of Iraq demonstrates to other potential proliferants some of the ways to defeat detection and verification through camouflage, concealment, and deceit. It will therefore be necessary to upgrade the technologies and other means to uncover clandestine nuclear activities and facilities to reestablish confidence of countries participating in the nuclear nonproliferation regime.

Notes

1. Much of the information in this section is based on Kathleen Bailey et al., "Iraq Inspections: Lesson Learned," US Defense Nuclear Agency Report No. DNA-TR-92-115, January, 1993. The report includes results from interviews by the author of thirty inspectors who served on one or more of the UNSCOM missions in Iraq from May 1991 through April 1992.

2. Testimony of David Kay before the US Senate Committee on Banking, October 27, 1992.

3. David Albright and Mark Hibbs, "Iraq and the Bomb: Were They Even Close?," *The Bulletin of Atomic Scientists*, March, 1991, p. 24.

4. David Albright and Mark Hibbs, "Hyping the Iraqi Bomb," *The Bulletin of Atomic Scientists*, March, 1991, pp. 26-28.

5. Jay C. Davis and David A. Kay, Letter to the Editor, *Physics Today*, February, 1993, p. 11.

6. Text reprinted in UN Doc. S/23514 (January 25, 1992) p. 20.

7. UN Doc. S/22986 (August 28, 1991) p. 19.

8. UN Doc. S/23165 (October 25, 1991) p. 21.

9. UNSCOM was responsible for the nuclear, chemical, biological, and missile teams sent into Iraq. IAEA participated only on the nuclear teams. Therefore, the designation given to the nuclear teams varies in number. This was the fourth team sent in by UNSCOM, but was only the second nuclear team.

10. The small quantities of plutonium separated would have been allowable under IAEA safeguards, had Iraq sought approval.

11. UN Doc. S/22788 (July 15, 1991) p. 7.

12. *The Washington Post*, October 31, 1992, p. A18.

13. Trevor Rowe, "UN Personnel's Safety Stirs Concern," *The Washington Post*, August 28, 1992, p. 28.

14. Michael Newlin, briefing on "Disarming Iraq: Preparing for the Long-Term Monitoring of Iraq's Nuclear Weapons Capability," Washington Council on Nonproliferation, October 26, 1992, p. 5.

15. Eric Schmitt, "UN Calls Off Inspections of Site, Iraq Put Off Limits," *The New York Times*, August 18, 1992, p. A1.

16. The quantity was insignificant and below the threshold for which the IAEA is on the lookout. The fact that Iraq was reprocessing, however, is important because it signals an intent to acquire weapons-usable plutonium from Iraqi spent fuel. Also, Iraq did not seek to exempt the materials, as it is required to do under safeguards.

17. R. James Woolsey, Testimony before the US Senate Committee on Governmental Affairs on "Proliferation Threats of the 1990s," February 24, 1993, p. 10 (mimeo)

18. Leon Barkho, "Watch on Iraq Urged," *The Washington Times*, March 8, 1993, p. A9.

5

The Changed
International Environment

In the late 1980s and early 1990s, changes in the international political environment were dramatic. The most significant events were the unification of formerly communist East Germany with West Germany, overthrow of communist regimes by several eastern European nations, dissolution of the Warsaw Pact, and the breakup of the Soviet Union. These events led to an easing of tensions and ended the Cold War. While US and former-Soviet nuclear arsenals remain, the threat of nuclear war has diminished. The new atmosphere led to the signing of the Strategic Arms Reduction Treaty (START I) as well as a follow-on agreement signed by Presidents Yeltsin and Bush just before the latter's departure from office (often referred to as START II).

Ironically, the very changes that have ended the Cold War have exacerbated the problems of nuclear proliferation. These problems, outlined below, present varying degrees of threat to international stability. Should any of them worsen in the near future, they could pose a major threat to extension of the NPT past 1995 and create new stimulus for proliferation worldwide.

Soviet Breakup May Yield New Nuclear Weapons States

A very serious question is whether three former Soviet republics now in possession of nuclear weapons—Ukraine, Belarus, and Kazakhstan—will give them up, leaving Russia as the sole inheritor of nuclear-weapon status. A related issue is whether any of the republics other than Russia will choose to pursue development and production of nuclear weapons. This second question will remain pertinent even if the three republics give up the former Soviet weapons on their soil.

When the breakup of the Soviet Union was announced in December 1991, over 7000 nuclear warheads were located in non-Russian republics. Moscow immediately ordered the return to Russia of all tactical nuclear weapons, which were more vulnerable to theft than strategic weapons because of their relatively small size and mobility. The strategic weapons, however, were not returned to Russian soil immediately. To do so would mean removing them from their role in the nuclear arsenal pointed at the United States. They would have had to be removed from their missile silos before replacement silos could be constructed in Russia. Even if replacement silos could have been prepared, it would not have been cost-effective because many of the strategic weapons were designated to be destroyed under the START I treaty then under negotiation.

Ukraine possesses 176 strategic missiles—130 SS-19s and 46 SS-24s—with over 1240 warheads. It also has 14 Bear-H and 16 Blackjack strategic bombers armed with 224 and 192 nuclear warheads respectively. Kazakhstan has 104 SS-18 missiles, each with 10 warheads, and an unknown number of nondeployed missiles. It also has 40 Bear-H bombers carrying a total of about 1400 nuclear weapons. Belarus has 72 road-mobile missiles, each with one warhead, and about 30 nondeployed intercontinental ballistic missiles.[1]

At the Alma–Ata Summit in December 1991, Ukraine and Belarus expressed willingness to give up the nuclear weapons and sign the NPT.[2] Ukraine also promised to give up its strategic nuclear weapons by the end of 1994. Kazakhstan made no similar commitments.

Kazakhstan President Nursultan Nazarbayev indicated his intention to maintain his country's nuclear weapon status. During a visit to New Delhi in February 1992, he said, "Kazakhstan supports the principle of parity in the question of elimination of nuclear weapons. Kazakhstan will be ready to eliminate its nuclear potential only on the condition if the United States, China, and Russia do the same."[3] Nazarbayev rejected pressures to sign the NPT as a "nonweapons state" saying, "Why does the United States not demand the same thing [signature of the NPT] from India and Pakistan that they do from us? Why for 30 years have France and England not taken part in nonproliferation? Why are you putting such pressure on Kazakhstan? This is incorrect."[4] Nazarbayev moved away from this position only when a security agreement had been signed with Moscow giving Kazakhstan a "nuclear umbrella," and a promise obtained from Washington that Kazakhstan would participate in negotiations on strategic arms. Nazarbayev then stated his country's intention to sign the NPT, but as a "republic on which nuclear weapons are temporarily located."

President Leonid Kravchuk announced on March 12, 1993, that Ukraine would stop the transfer of tactical nuclear weapons to Russia, saying that their destruction should be conducted under international control.[5] At a summit of republics in Kiev eight days later, Ukraine blocked an agreement to ratify START I, refusing to recognize Russia as the only successor nuclear weapon state.

Despite protests, the republics with nuclear weapons remaining on their soil signed the Lisbon Protocol in May 1992, following significant diplomatic pressure by the United States. The protocol is a document designed to update START I by taking account of the newly independent states formed from the former Soviet Union. (The START treaty was signed in July 1991, before the breakup.) It made Belarus, Kazakhstan, Ukraine, and Russia parties to START I and obliged the first three to "adhere to the Treaty on the Non-Proliferation of Nuclear Weapons of July 1, 1968 as non-nuclear-weapon-state parties in the shortest possible time, and shall begin immediately to take all necessary actions to this end in accordance with their constitutional practices."[6]

To obtain Ukraine's signature on the protocol, Washington made major concessions. One concession could result in neutralizing the vows to join the NPT. The flaw is that the protocol accords Ukraine, Kazakhstan, and Belarus equal status with Russia in the ratification and implementation of the obligations of START and recognizes all four former Soviet republics as "successors" of the Soviet Union. "The Protocol denies any special right for Russia regarding Soviet strategic weapons and stipulates that Russia must negotiate arrangements concerning the ceilings and limitations imposed by START with Ukraine and the other two republics. Thus, nuclear weapons may remain on the territories of these states even after the START reductions. In fact, this might be used by Ukraine and others to claim not only de facto, but also de jure nuclear status."[7]

Kazakhstan ratified START I (with the condition that entry into force be dependent on ratification by the other three nuclear republics) and agreed gradually to give up nuclear weapons on its soil, without making demands for compensation or security guarantees. Belarus also renounced nuclear ambitions and ratified START I.

Although Belarus may move to give up its nuclear option quickly, Kazakhstan may not denuclearize unless Ukraine does. Ukraine has begun to backpedal on its earlier commitment to become nonnuclear, primarily because the Ukraine leadership realized that the nuclear weapons on its soil are worth political capital and, perhaps, hard currency. This perception was generated, in part, by the fact that the US Congress had just allocated $400 million for the safe, secure destruction of weapons from the former Soviet Union (later expanded to $800 million) and was negotiating to buy 500 tons of enriched uranium removed from Russian weapons at a price of $5 to 15,000 per kilogram.

When Ukraine signed the protocol, the three non-Russian republics delivered letters to President Bush stating that they would destroy all nuclear weapons within seven years. This obviated the earlier promise made at Alma–Ata to destroy them by 1994. Then followed a series of signals that Ukraine might not be willing to destroy them at all. In October 1992, the Ukrainian parliament rejected a draft non-nuclear-military doctrine presented by Defense Minister Konstantin Morozov. During the debate, some deputies demanded that nuclear weapons be kept as a deterrent.[8] Soon thereafter, First Deputy Prime Minister Igor Yuchovsky said that the enriched uranium in weapons located in Ukraine should be worth $5 to 6 billion.[9] (Actually, its market value is only about $180 million.) He said, "We can sell these nuclear warheads to the highest bidder...to nuclear states, that means Russia first of all, or maybe another state, depending on which pays most."[10] Ukrainian Prime Minister Leonid Kuchma expressed similar feelings: "We removed tactical weapons from Ukraine and what did we get in exchange?"[11]

By early December 1992, Ukraine had refined and expanded its demands. Foreign Minister Anatoly Zlenko told US Secretary of State Lawrence Eagleburger that Ukraine would not ratify the START agreement or join the NPT until several concrete issues were resolved. Specifically, the demands were: Ukraine's international security must be guaranteed; it must receive financial support for dismantling and storing nuclear weapons on Ukrainian soil; compensation for uranium and plutonium removed from weapons must be paid; and there must be an accord with Russia on sharing such compensation.[12] Meanwhile, Ukraine moved to consolidate physical control over the weapons by requiring the soldiers guarding the bases where they are kept to declare loyalty to Ukraine over Russia, and assuming responsibility for providing the soldiers' food, pay, and housing.[13] Although Ukraine may not yet be able to retarget the missiles in its possession, Premier Leonid Kuchma has claimed that Ukraine has the technical capability to do so.[14]

Responding to Ukraine's concerns, President Bush wrote to Ukrainian President Leonid Kravchuk to offer $175 million in assistance if his country becomes party to the NPT and ratifies START.[15] Ukrainian officials continued to balk at the idea of signing the NPT. The chairman of the Foreign Relations Committee of the Ukraine parliament said on March 19 (after meeting with top Russian and Ukraine official), "We do not intend to accede to the NPT and we will ratify START only under certain conditions."[16]

There are at least four dangers to international nonproliferation policy associated with the events summarized above. First, there is a distinct possibility that any of the three republics may decide to retain the nuclear weapons remaining within their territory and under their physical control. This may not be done in a clear-cut, definitive manner. Rather, the republics may say nothing and fail to implement political commitments.

Second, there is the possibility that the currently possessed weapons will be transferred to Russia, but one or more of the republics will choose to develop and produce nuclear weapons independently. Ukraine and Kazakhstan have talented, experienced technologists as well as facilities potentially useful for nuclear weapons development. Ukraine has 14 unsafeguarded nuclear power reactors in operation; Kazakhstan, one—a breeder reactor (which produces plutonium) in operation since 1973.[17] Kazakhstan has a nuclear test site. For missiles and space, Ukraine has the plant that has been sole producer of the SS-18 ICBM and SL-16 space launch vehicle and a facility for final assembly of the SS-24 ICBM.[18] Kazakhstan has facilities which produce short-range ballistic missiles and missile components, as well as a space-launch facility. (See Table 2.) While an investment of time and money would be required to make nuclear weapons, each of the republics has more infrastructure than did Pakistan or Iraq when they started their weapons programs.

Third, if insistence by Ukraine leads to weapons dismantlement in the republics, it will raise the prospect of theft by terrorists or retention of the materials by the republics. The United States and Russia have worked to dissuade the republics from insisting on in-country dismantlement, but the issue may again arise.

A fourth danger is that nuclear weapons will be used so effectively to bargain for political and economic concessions that they will become a recognized bartering tool. Not only are Belarus and Kazakhstan carefully monitoring Ukraine's "negotiations" over its weapons, but others are watching as well. In the future, proliferant nations may use concessions gained by Ukraine as a precedent for exacting their own price for giving up nuclear weapons.

Nuclear Materials May Be Sold to Terrorists

Nuclear weapons—or the components and materials from them—can be sold for high sums to terrorists or proliferant nations. Sales of spent nuclear fuel, a source of plutonium, may also be lucrative. If a nation, subnational group, or individual were to market such materials, they could be used to make nuclear or radiological weapons. (The latter are designed to disperse deadly radioactive materials.)

Numerous reports of nuclear smuggling followed the breakup of the former Soviet Union and the Warsaw Pact. Senator Sam Nunn learned during a trip to Belarus that a plot to smuggle uranium to Poland had been thwarted.[19] Many people, mostly East Europeans, have been arrested trying to sell materials such as tiny flakes of plutonium or several pounds of lightly enriched uranium. In Germany alone, more than 100 cases of such smuggling were investigated in the first three quarters of 1992, up from 29 total cases in 1991.[20] Most of those arrested were figures known to be involved in organized crime, using established smuggling operations for a "new" product, nuclear materials. However, there are some who are officials or military personnel. Some of the nuclear materials originated in the former

TABLE 2 Nuclear Profiles of Newly Independent States

COUNTRY	Nuclear Weapons	Nuclear Power Reactor	Nuclear Research Reactor	Nuclear Weapons Design	Uranium Mining, Milling	Uranium Enrichment Capability	Fuel Fabrication Facility	Plutonium Production, Handling	Heavy Water Production	Nuclear Research Center	Nuclear Test Site	Acceded To NPT
Armenia		a							e	x		
Azerbaijan												x
Belarus	x		x							x		h
Estonia					x							x
Georgia			b							x		
Kazakhstan	x	x	x		x		x	d		x	x	
Kyrgyzstan					x							
Latvia			x							x		x
Lithuania		x										x
Moldova						c						
Russia	x	x	x	x	x	x	x	x	x	x	x	x
Tadjikistan					x				x			
Turkmenistan												
Ukraine	x	x	x	i	x				x	x		
Uzbekistan			x		x					x		x

a. The two Armenian reactors were shut down in 1989 for safety reasons, but the Armenian government has announced its intent to restart them.
b. The IRT-M Tbilisi was shut down in 1990.
c. A uranium enrichment facility, of at least an experimental nature, probably operated at Navoi during the 1970s and 1980s.
d. A hot cell is reportedly located at the Semipalatinsk test site.
e. Although one report of an Armenian heavy-water site has appeared in print, there has been no additional confirmation.
f. The Ulbinsky Metallurgy Plant in Ust-Kamenogorsk produces beryllium and possibly zirconium.
g. Zirconium, halfnium, and ion-exchange resins are produced in Ukraine at the Pridneprovsky Chemical Factory.
h. The Belarusian Parliament approved accession to the NPT on February 4, 1993, but as of March 31, 1993, had not deposited its instrument of accession.
i. Based on discussion by Kathleen Bailey with a knowledgeable Russian nuclear official.

Source: Based on information from William C. Potter, *Nuclear Profiles of the Soviet Successor States* (forthcoming, 1993). Used with permission by author.

Soviet Union.[21] A CIA official confirmed that some enriched uranium and small amounts of plutonium were smuggled out of the former Soviet Union.[22]

Thus far, none of the known smuggling attempts have involved significant amounts of materials that could be used to make weapons. In the future, the situation may become more dangerous, in part, because nuclear weapons may not be transferred to Russia from three possessor-republics. Perhaps more important, however, is the fact that reactor fuel remaining in the former Soviet republics and eastern Europe may be sold. Several former Soviet republics have either research or power reactors: Latvia, Lithuania, Belarus, Ukraine, Georgia, Armenia, Russia, and Kazakhstan. There are also many nuclear reactors in eastern Europe, the fuel for which is no longer being returned to Russia for storage. Reprocessing technology to remove the plutonium from spent fuel is well documented in public literature, and the equipment and expertise required are widely available.

More Scientist-Mercenaries May Market Skills

The end of the Cold War has brought about promises of drastic reductions in the nuclear arsenals of Russia and the United States, as well as postponement or cancellation of expansion and modernization of some French nuclear weapons. As a result, budget priorities are being shifted. Russian and US weapons programs are being cut and workers laid off. This has prompted a widespread concern about the potential of a Russian "brain drain" in which key scientists and technicians would sell their expertise to the highest bidder. And, the problem may be even broader, involving technical experts from the non-Russian republics. As CIA Director James Woolsey testified in February 1993, "...a substantial number of former Soviet scientists involved in weapons of mass destruction research and development are of Ukrainian origin, so the risk of leakage and brain drain is not simply a Russian problem."[23]

To lessen the chances of an outflow of Russian scientist-mercenaries, Russia, the United States, and Germany formed an International Science and Technology Center in February 1992. The United States provided $25 million, as did the European Community and Japan. Canada also pledged contributions. The center provides funding for former-Soviet scientists to work on a variety of projects, including nuclear waste disposal, weapons-complex cleanup, and other ventures. Other projects have also been initiated to employ scientists from the nuclear sector. For example, the US Department of Energy signed a contract in 1992 to hire 116 Russian scientists to work on nuclear fusion research.

While there is a danger of former Soviet experts selling their services to other countries or to terrorists, the problem is actually much larger. In fact, there may be even greater danger that US nationals will begin to market their skills elsewhere. Americans, in general, are more self-sufficient and aggressive about finding a job than their former-Soviet counterparts, who depended on the state to provide them with employment. Also, English-speakers are likely to be able to market their skills more effectively and broadly. There is also the likelihood that American scientists will have been exposed to a greater proportion of the weapons program on which they worked than a Soviet national because the Soviet Union compartmentalized weapons programs to a greater extent to maintain secrecy and security. A US computer expert, for example, might have more knowledge of weapons-design information than would a Soviet computer expert.

The problem of scientist-mercenaries is not limited to the superpowers. South Africa had a nuclear weapons program and gave it up in 1992, after producing a significant quantity of enriched uranium and building six nuclear weapons. South African scientists and technicians might look for jobs doing what they know best in other countries such as Israel or Taiwan. While there are no publicly known precedents in the nuclear arena for such behavior, there is one example of a weapons designer from a less developed country taking employment with a proliferant country. The former director of Brazil's Aerospace Technology Center, disappointed when his country abandoned attempts to develop an intermediate-range ballistic missile, went to Iraq to lead a team attempting to improve Saddam Hussein's Scuds.[24]

Dissolution of Security Pacts
May Promote Weapons Programs

One of the most significant changes in the international political environ-ment is the diminution of the role of security pacts. The Warsaw Pact is now dissolved and the North Atlantic Treaty Organization (NATO) is undergo-ing drastic change and a lessening of its security role. These changes have important repercussions which may stimulate proliferation tendencies in Europe.

One effect is that nations party to these pacts find themselves in a position whereby they are no longer protected against external aggressors and, perhaps more importantly, their neighbors and fellow-pact members. They may now reassess whether their defense and security interests would be better served by developing their own nuclear deterrent. One nation already has suggested this. Ukrainian leaders say that a principal reason they need nuclear weapons is to deter Russia. The strong support in Ukraine for retaining nuclear weapons has surprised many observers who thought that anti-nuclear sentiment there would be prohibitively strong.

The Chernobyl accident affected the Ukraine territory and population dramatically, but not so much that nuclear weapons are rejected as an option.

Nations in NATO may also reconsider nuclear weapons possession. With most nuclear weapons being removed from NATO, the US nuclear arsenal being reduced, US nuclear testing diminished (which may reduce reliability), and NATO devolving, will Germany or others in the future want their own nuclear deterrent?

A second effect of the reduced role of security pacts is the freedom that it gives individual nations, or leaders within them, to make decisions about developing national military capabilities. Previously, if a national military contemplated developing its own nuclear forces, it almost certainly would have been found out by others in the pact and stopped. This is similar to the role played by the pacts in deterring intrapact fighting. The civil war in the former Yugoslavia, for example, would probably have been precluded during the Cold War days, and the division of Czechoslovakia into two ethnic-based nations would have been stymied. Now that there is no superpower dominating the decision-making processes in European countries (East and West) and the former Soviet republics, there may be greater freedom to decide on developing an independent nuclear capability.

Conclusion

Some of the greatest challenges to the nuclear nonproliferation regime have resulted from the radically changed international political environment of the early 1990s. Whereas in the past, the primary proliferation concerns stemmed from the less developed countries of the so-called Third World, today there are new problem-countries. The republics of the former Soviet Union—particularly Ukraine, Belarus, and Kazakhstan—possess former-Soviet strategic nuclear weapons and may not give them up. Even if they do send them to Russia, these republics have the capacity themselves to develop weapons independently, as do some of the nations of eastern and western Europe.

There is also danger that nuclear materials, equipment, and technical know-how will be sold to terrorists or proliferant nations. The "brain drain" problem is not Russia's alone; it is a problem of many countries with weapons programs, especially the former Soviet Union and the United States.

Coincident with the increasing availability of technology and materials is the possible growth in incentive for proliferation. The disintegration of security pacts in Europe may stimulate new fears as well as remove old constraints on independent defense decision making.

Notes

1. These figures are compiled from numerous sources, including the public declarations by Moscow pursuant to the START Treaty.

2. This summit meeting was held by the three original founders of the Commonwealth of Independent States—Belarus, Russia, and Ukraine—and attended by Kazakhstan, Moldova, Armenia, Azerbaijan, and four Central Asian republics. The primary purpose was to discuss common defense affairs.

3. *Izvestiya*, February 24, 1992, as quoted in Sergei Rogov et al., "Commonwealth Defense Arrangements and International Security," Paper by the Institute of USA and Canada and the Center for Naval Analyses, 1992, p. 21.

4. Michael Dobbs, "Kazakh Sets Conditions on A-Arms," *The Washington Post*, May 6, 1992, pp. A1, A20.

5. *Kraznaya Zvezda*, March 14, 1992 and *Izvestiya*, March 13, 1992, as quoted in Sergei Rogov et al., "Commonwealth Defense Arrangements," pp. 18-19.

6. Article V of the "Protocol to the Treaty Between the United States of America and the Union of Soviet Socialist Republics on the Reduction and Limitation of Strategic Offensive Arms."

7. Rogov et al., op. cit., p.24.

8. Mark Frankland, "Ukraine's Stance on Nuclear Arsenal Stirs Fresh Worries," *The Washington Times*, November 23, 1992, p. A7.

9. Fred Kaplan, "Ukraine Officials Tying Missile Removal to Aid," *Boston Globe*, November 16, 1992, p. 1.

10. Associated Press, "Ukraine Might Not Give Missiles to Russia, But Auction Them Off," *Valley Times*, (Pleasanton, CA) November 6, 1992, p. 3B.

11. Ibid.

12. "Ukraine Delays on Arms Pacts," *The Washington Post*, December 16, 1992, p. A36.

13. R. Jeffrey Smith, "Officials See Shift in Ukraine's Nuclear Position," *The Washington Post*, December 19, 1992, p. A10.

14. Daniel Sneider, "Russia, Ukraine Stalemated in Arms Talks," *The Christian Science Monitor*, March 8, 1993, p. 6.

15. Don Oberdorfer, "Bush Offers $175 Million for Nonnuclear Ukraine," *The Washington Post*, December 10, 1992, p. A12.

16. Associated Press report March 19, 1993.

17. William C. Potter, "Nuclear Exports From the Former Soviet Union: What's New, What's True," *Arms Control Today*, January/February, 1993, p. 5.

18. Central Intelligence Agency, "The Defense Industries of the Newly Independent States of Eurasia," January 1993, Document OSE 93-10001, p. 5.

19. Don Oberdorfer, "Russian Strife Seen Straining Arms Controls," *The Washington Post*, February 4, 1993, p. A11.

20. Steve Coll, "For Sale: Nuclear Contraband," *The Washington Post*, November 29, 1992, p. A1.

21. For example, the 14 pounds of uranium involved in an attempted black-market sale by three Poles was believed to have come from a former Soviet Republic. See "Poles Arrested For Smuggling Uranium," *The Washington Times*, March 8, 1993, p. A2.

22. Bill Gertz, "Sensitive Technology Leaks Blamed on Soviet Breakup," *The Washington Times,* February 25, 1993, p. A5.

23. R. James Woolsey, Testimony before the US Senate Committee on Governmental Affairs, February 24, 1993, p. 6 of mimeo.

24. Thomas Kamm, "Brazilian Arms Experts Said To Upgrade Iraq's Missiles," *The Wall Street Journal,* August 30, 1990, p. 5.

6

Disarmament

Article VI of the Nuclear Nonproliferation Treaty requires parties "...to pursue negotiations in good faith on effective measures relating to cessation of the nuclear arms race at an early date and to nuclear disarmament, and on a treaty on general and complete disarmament under strict and effective international control." This treaty obligation codifies the basic premise that nuclear disarmament by the nuclear weapon states is a key to successful nuclear nonproliferation policy. Simply put, the logic is that if the "haves" give up their nuclear weapons, the "have nots" will no longer seek them. By disarming, the nuclear weapon states would provide an example for proliferants and potential proliferants to follow. Specifically, it is argued that disarmament would have at least two positive effects. First, nuclear-weapon possession would be discredited and would no longer be a means to acquire prestige. Second, proliferants would have no reason to seek nuclear weapons as a deterrent against nuclear weapon states.

This chapter discusses reasons why some arguments linking disarmament and nuclear nonproliferation are in error. It also addresses the reasons why total nuclear disarmament is dangerous and impractical. A case is made for the notion that nonproliferation policy actually can be damaged by the linkage with disarmament.

Disarmament Does Not Promote Nonproliferation

The link between the propensity to proliferate and the unwillingness of the nuclear weapon states to disarm is weak. Disarmament would not negate the already-limited prestige value of nuclear weapons. Proliferants, with the exception of India vis-à-vis China, do not seek nuclear weapons to deter nuclear use by the five declared nuclear weapon states. Most nations seeking nuclear weapons want them to deter nuclear threats from other proliferants (i.e., not one of the five declared nuclear weapon states) or conventional threats. Some states may also seek such weapons for hegemonistic goals or for prestige value. Thus, even if nuclear-weapon states were to disarm, it would not affect the motives of proliferant states. These points deserve further elaboration.

The Value of Nuclear Weapons Is Eroding

To some extent, the presumption that nuclear weapons have prestige value is based on a false foundation. The first five nuclear weapon states were extremely powerful militarily, politically, and technologically *prior* to acquiring nuclear weapons, and their abilities to develop nuclear weapons stemmed from that power. This is not to say that nuclear weapons did not enhance the prestige and power of the five, but the weapons were not the origin of their power. Historically, however, this point has not been acknowledged by many countries.

In the 1950s and 1960s, representatives of less developed countries frequently enunciated their view that nuclear weapons were a means to political power. One of the most frequently cited examples was that the five countries accorded permanent status on the United Nations Security Council were the same as the five nuclear weapon states. In reality, the cause and effect in this example is mistaken. The permanent members of the security council were chosen *before* those five nations acquired nuclear weapons.

Some nations have also claimed that nuclear weapon status has been frequently used by the United States and others to augment their political clout. For example, India has claimed that the United States implied a nuclear threat against India in 1971, the year that upheaval in then-East Pakistan led to the formation of Bangladesh.

While there may have been instances when the nuclear weapon capabilities of the United States and others influenced political events, there are few if any clear-cut examples. In fact, there are many examples of crises and problems in which nuclear weapon possession was of no help. The Vietnam War provided the most telling example of a situation in which the United States could not use its nuclear weapons, even though defeat appeared imminent. Subsequently, the United States faced multiple instances of terrorism, hostage holding, and military attack. In one example, many Americans were killed in the bombing of the US Marine barracks in Beirut, Lebanon, in 1983, and the United States was forced to diminish its presence in the region or face further casualties. Still, Washington's nuclear weapon status was of no practical use. Likewise, the former Soviet Union was faced with military defeat in Afghanistan, and did not resort to nuclear threats or use.

Over time, it has become evident that nuclear weapons in the hands of responsible states are useful as a deterrent to other nuclear weapon states, but afford little use in other political–military crises. The prestige value of nuclear weapons has diminished, in part, because of the realization that these weapons cannot be used for many functions other than deterrence; the social, political, and environmental repercussions are so great that their use by any responsible nation lacks credibility in almost any imaginable scenario.

Even proliferant states have given evidence that the prestige value of nuclear weapons has diminished. Following the open weapons testing by the five nuclear states, at least four other nations developed nuclear capabilities. India, Israel, Pakistan, and South Africa all acquired the materials and technology to make weapons. India even tested a device in 1974 and South Africa admitted in 1993 having constructed and then destroyed six nuclear weapons. It is also possible that Israel tested a nuclear device in 1979, when US satellites picked up data indicating a probable nuclear test took place in the South Atlantic. Despite their technological achievement of nuclear weapon status, three of these states' nuclear capabilities remain "in the closet," and one has renounced nuclear weapons, never having admitted possession until after destruction. The benefits of nonadmission outweigh the potential prestige to be gained by open acknowledgment.

The value placed on nuclear weapons has been further eroded by another phenomenon: Today tremendous political and economic power can be wielded by nations that have no significant military capabilities and no nuclear weapons. In fact, the absence of costly military and weapons programs may be a significant factor in the growth of these nations' economic power. Japan and Germany are two examples of states that acquired extraordinary prestige and influence without having developed nuclear weapons.

Even though no one-to-one correlation exists between great power status and nuclear weapon possession, nuclear weapons probably will always have an appeal. The fact is that nuclear weapons are extremely powerful and threatening, and are relatively inexpensive to maintain. They can be used politically or militarily by any nation which has them and is willing to use them for more than deterrence. As will be explained later in this chapter, this appeal will likely be strengthened if disarmament were ever to occur. This is because one or a few nuclear weapons, in the hands of a nation willing to use them, become even more potent a threat in an environment in which potential adversaries have zero nuclear weapons.

In conclusion, the prestige-value of nuclear weapons is eroding. Nevertheless, given the massive destructive power of nuclear weapons, they will always provide the possessor with some level of political and military power. Even if the nuclear weapon states were to give up their arsenals, nuclear weapons would still be recognized as a means to extraordinary power.

Disarmament Does Not Alter Proliferants' Real Motives

Some argue that nuclear disarmament by the five declared nuclear weapon states is necessary to remove an important threat against non-nuclear-weapon states. Doing so hypothetically will remove the incentive for non-nuclear-weapon states to develop their own nuclear deterrent. The central problem with this argument is that proliferant countries do not pursue nuclear weapons to have a deterrent against nuclear arsenals of the five declared nuclear weapons states. (The exception to this is the case of India, which said it developed nuclear weapons primarily as a response to China.) At least three points undermine linkage between disarmament by the five and proliferation by others:

1. The declared nuclear weapons states are very unlikely to use nuclear weapons to threaten states not in possession of weapons of mass destruction, or in military alliance with a nuclear weapons state.

During the 1960s, as the Nuclear Nonproliferation Treaty was being crafted, the nuclear weapons of the five possessor nations were seen as very threatening. Non-nuclear-weapons states wanted the five to guarantee that nuclear weapons would not be used to pressure or attack them; they wanted negative security assurances (discussed in Chapter 1). Without such assurances, the non-nuclear-weapons states argued that they would need to retain the nuclear option so they could develop their own nuclear deterrent. The nuclear weapons states agreed to give negative security assurances.

In the intervening years, the declared nuclear-weapons states have lived up to their obligations to refrain from using their weapons politically or militarily vis-à-vis non-nuclear-weapons states. In crisis after crisis, none of the five nuclear weapon states have threatened to use or used their weapons, and over time, less developed countries have learned that the declared five nuclear weapons states pose little or no nuclear threat to them.

To some extent, the policy of negative security assurances should serve to dampen motives of nations to acquire nuclear weapons. Once nations proliferate, they become potential nuclear targets for the declared nuclear weapon states because the negative security assurance no longer applies.

In the future, there may be another reason for the declared nuclear weapon states to refuse to extend a negative security assurance: if a proliferant develops other types of weapons of mass destruction, chemical or biological. France, the United Kingdom, and the United States have all given up chemical and biological weapons and forsworn their use.[1] Thus, they may rely on nuclear weapons as a deterrent against chemical and biological threats.[2] By refusing to rule out retaliation with nuclear weapons if Saddam Hussein used weapons of mass destruction, President Bush may have been employing an implicit nuclear threat.[3]

2. New nuclear weapons states cannot match the arsenals of the declared nuclear weapons states.

Even if a proliferant country were to devote all of its resources to nuclear weapons acquisition, it would be unable to match the arsenals of any of the five declared nuclear weapon states—either in quantitative or qualitative terms.

Sweden is an example of a nation that actually began a nuclear weapons program for the purpose of deterring a nuclear weapons state (the USSR) and then abandoned it.[4] Historical records detail the Swedish debate. Although financial considerations played a significant role, the crucial argument by the military against the idea of acquiring weapons was that they would not be effective against the overwhelming arsenals of the most likely nuclear foe.

Thus, the five acknowledged nuclear weapons states are very unlikely to threaten non-nuclear-weapons states (with nuclear weapons) and, if they were interested in threatening a proliferant nation, they probably would not be deterred by the proliferant's very limited nuclear capabilities. It is quite possible, however, that a misguided leader like Iraq's Saddam Hussein may *think* that a limited, low-technology nuclear arsenal can be useful. In the case of such leaders, they will be motivated to get nuclear weapons regardless of whether or not the five nuclear weapons states disarm. In fact, disarmament by the five may offer an incentive to rogue leaders, who may perceive that their limited-size arsenals will be more effective in the face of vastly reduced nuclear forces in the five possessor states.

3. Nuclear weapons of a proliferant nation may be used to deter conventional threats.

Nuclear weapons are a means of deterring overwhelming conventional threats—including those posed by the five declared nuclear weapons states. For example, had Saddam Hussein possessed nuclear weapons, the Desert Storm coalition might never have formed. As was clear from the debate in the United States over whether to oust Iraq from Kuwait, a central concern was whether Iraq possessed weapons of mass destruction. And, in the future, the United States is likely to hesitate to send conventionally armed troops into conflicts which may turn nuclear.

If a nation is motivated to obtain nuclear arms because it wants to deter US or other conventional forces, nuclear disarmament by the five declared states will not reduce the chances of nuclear proliferation. In fact, nuclear disarmament may make proliferation even more attractive because it will eliminate the possibility that a proliferant's nuclear arms can be countered or deterred.

Total Disarmament Is Impractical

The link between disarmament and nonproliferation is clearly stated in Article VI of the Nuclear Nonproliferation Treaty, cited above. Essentially, this is the quid pro quo for other nations agreeing to foreswear nuclear weapons.

Despite the language in the NPT and the beliefs of disarmament advocates, nuclear disarmament by the nuclear weapons states is neither a practical nor realistic measure. And, it is highly unlikely to have much impact on the motivations of proliferants.

Getting rid of nuclear weapons is more difficult than foregoing the option in the first place. Nations that have already decided that their security interests are better served by nuclear weapons possession are unlikely to reverse that position unless they can be persuaded that nuclear weapons actually decrease rather than increase their security. Sweden and South Africa are two examples of nations that did reverse their decision to acquire nuclear weapons. Sweden decided that it could never match the arsenals of some potential adversaries and stopped its program before culmination. South Africa did build nuclear weapons, but destroyed them when it no longer felt threatened by Soviet-backed adversaries on its borders and when it became apparent that the white government would have to cede political power to the nonwhite majority.

In the case of the United States and Russia, total nuclear disarmament is highly unlikely in the near or midterm future, although both will continue to identify the concept as a goal in an ideal world. There are at least two reasons that both will continue to view nuclear weapons possession to be in their national security interests. First, nuclear weapons are central to providing security to allies, obviating the need for those countries to develop their own nuclear arsenals. For example, as long as NATO has a nuclear umbrella, Germany is less likely to perceive a need for or have the freedom to develop its own nuclear arsenal. Russia's nuclear umbrella over Kazakhstan obviates arguments that might be made in that country's political circles for retaining or developing nuclear weapons.

A second reason that nuclear weapons will almost certainly remain in the arsenals of the United States and Russia (as well as others) is the unwillingness to disarm unilaterally. Neither nation can ever be sure that the other has given up its nuclear weapons, even if the other offers promises that it has. There is absolutely no technology—existing or on scientists' drawing boards—that would enable one country to know that the other does not have hidden nuclear weapons, materials, or components of weapons. This is why superpower arms control measures have focused primarily on "observable" delivery systems, such as the missiles covered by the Intermediate Nuclear Forces Treaty. Even if verification measures are developed to give a nation confidence that an adversary is indeed destroying dismantled warheads, for example, there can never be convincing assurance that there are no undeclared weapons. An arsenal of hundreds of weapons could easily be hidden by one nation while the other eliminates its arsenal. The nation with hidden arms could then overwhelm the disarmed nation.

Notes

1. China is believed to continue its biological weapons program and Russia, its chemical and biological weapons programs. See US Arms Control & Disarmament Agency, "Adherence To and Compliance With Arms Control Agreements and The President's Report To Congress on Soviet Noncompliance With Arms Control Agreements," January 14, 1993, pp. 13, 14.

2. This point was made by Dr. Graham Pearson, Director General of the United Kingdom's Chemical and Biological Defence Establishment, in the television program *Newsnight* (British Broadcasting Corporation 2, on January 21, 1993).

3. This argument is made by McGeorge Bundy in "Nuclear Weapons and the Gulf," *Foreign Affairs*, Fall, 1991, p. 84.

4. A description of the Swedish program is contained in Kathleen Bailey's *Doomsday Weapons in the Hands of Many* (Urbana: University of Illinois Press, 1991), pp. 30-32.

7

End Nuclear Testing?

Many proponents of nuclear nonproliferation advocate a Comprehensive Test Ban (CTB). Principal arguments are that a CTB would: (a) reduce proliferant's motives to acquire nuclear weapons; (b) prevent modernization and improvement of nuclear weapons, thus contributing to disarmament; and (c) fulfill an obligation of nuclear weapons states party to the Nuclear Nonproliferation Treaty (NPT), which will strengthen the treaty regime. Some also add that the United States and Russia should lead the way by ending nuclear testing first, which will be a symbol of their commitment to nonproliferation and provide a "model" for others to follow. This chapter will discuss these arguments, as well as the reasons for nuclear testing.

Reasons for Nuclear Testing

The question of whether there should be a CTB may become a moot point. France and Russia declared a temporary moratorium on nuclear testing. In 1992, the United States placed new limits on its nuclear testing. First, President Bush announced that no nuclear tests would be conducted for new weapons designs or force modernization; US testing will be conducted only to improve weapons safety, security, and reliability. Later that year, the US Congress enacted legislation allowing only 15 nuclear tests, which must be conducted prior to 1996, each limited to the purpose of improving safety or proving reliability. These moves have been taken for a number of reasons, including economics and a desire by many in the Congress to ready the United States for a CTB. The greatest incentive to reduce or end testing, however, stems from the end of the Cold War. As threats have diminished, so has the need for new nuclear weapons or larger stockpiles.

Yet, proponents of nuclear testing argue that it should continue, despite the end of the Cold War and the planned reductions in superpower arsenals by over one-half in 1990s. The principal reasons are to ensure nuclear weapons safety, reliability, and survivability. There is also need to develop techniques that will render ineffective a terrorist or proliferant-nation nuclear device. And, without nuclear testing, it will be extremely difficult to maintain a cadre of weapons experts—people who will maintain the nuclear deterrent for as long as we depend on it for our security.

Safety

The reliance of the United States and Russia on their nuclear arsenals for national security is unlikely to end in the near future, as is discussed in Chapter 5. The weapons that remain in the stockpiles of both nations should be as safe as practically and technically possible. They should be resistant to fire and damage from other types of accidents. There should be the minimum possibility that they will detonate and spread nuclear materials, or that there will be a nuclear yield in event of accident.

Over the past 40 years, there have been several accidents involving nuclear weapons. In a few of these, the high explosives detonated, spreading nuclear materials but not causing a nuclear explosion. These occurrences led to an increased emphasis on developing and using insensitive high explosives, less likely to detonate in violent accidents. Other safety improvements include improved electrical systems that cannot be affected by spurious electrical signals such as lightning and fire-resistant pits that encase a bomb's plutonium core to reduce the risk of dispersal in an accident.

An independent, Congressionally appointed panel chaired by Dr. Sidney Drell was asked to evaluate the safety of the US nuclear stockpile. The Drell Panel's December 1990 report called for enhanced safety measures to be incorporated into nuclear weapons that are to remain in the enduring stockpile, a process which the panel acknowledged would require further nuclear testing.

Reliability

There must also be assurance that the weapons will work; they must be reliable. While there can be significant information and confidence gained from nonnuclear testing and modeling, these means are not sufficient with current levels of technology. There have been instances when nuclear testing has revealed flaws that were not discovered by other means.[1] One-third of the weapons designs put in the stockpile since 1958 have required nuclear tests to detect problems and/or evaluate corrective measures. Since 1975, five of eleven nuclear weapons designs have required nuclear testing to identify and resolve problems after weapon deployment. The following is taken from a 1992 US government white paper on nuclear testing:[2]

Since 1958 the United States has deployed forty-one different nuclear weapon systems. Of these, fourteen nuclear weapon systems needed corrective modifications after they were deployed or were ready for deployment because deficiencies were either discovered or evaluated in subsequent nuclear tests. For example, a final proof test at a warhead's low-temperature extreme was conducted after the warhead had entered production. The warhead, developed for the air-launched cruise missile, was scheduled for deployment in the mid-1980's. The test results were a complete surprise. The warhead exploded with only a tiny fraction of its design yield. The weapon had been tested extensively in non-nuclear hydrodynamic tests, even at the low-temperature extreme, with no indication of trouble. A design change to a much more conservative system was made to the warhead, and the warhead was successfully tested a year later.

The nuclear warhead for the Army's Sergeant Missile was designed during the 1958-61 test moratorium, so its design was based on non-nuclear hydrodynamics tests and on computer-design calculations. It was fielded in April 1962. Because the warhead design was based on a successful warhead tested earlier, there was great confidence that the Sergeant warhead would perform as expected. *When the warhead was finally tested, however, it gave only a fraction of its expected yield, a yield so small that it was militarily ineffective. Scientists were able to correct the design fault and test a redesigned (and successful) warhead within three months of the nuclear test that discovered the problem. This example dramatically illustrates the limitations and perils of having to modify warhead designs based on non nuclear testing and computer calculations alone.*

[emphasis added]

Note that there are instances when new designs are based on old ones, and the device did not operate as expected. Although there are to be no new, modern designs for the US stockpile, this point has relevance. For example, a design problem may be found that requires a change in the device design after a weapon is in the stockpile. There may be a lack of confidence in the workability of the device after those changes unless the redesign can be tested. And, even "small" changes designed to improve safety or security of weapons can lead to unanticipated problems with the workability of the design—problems that might not be detected via nonnuclear testing. Continued nuclear testing assures that the weapons work as planned, without adverse effects from storage and aging.

Survivability

Deterrence depends on convincing the adversary that retaliation is credible. The leadership in another nuclear weapons state must not be allowed to think that US nuclear forces can be rendered ineffective by a first strike. It is therefore important that US military systems can operate in a nuclear environment. This means that US nuclear delivery systems—and the command-and-control systems upon which their performance depends—must operate during and after exposure to nuclear effects.

The United States is continually working to improve its defenses such as those intended to track and destroy incoming missiles and aircraft. It is also modernizing conventional capabilities such as the precision weapons used so effectively in Desert Storm to attack facilities without undue loss of civilians. It is important that some of these defenses and advanced conventional capabilities can operate in a nuclear-disturbed environment. Nuclear testing is required to assure these systems will operate under such exposure; the requisite testing cannot be simulated.[3]

Some may inquire, "Why are nuclear weapons not designed to be safe, secure, and reliable from the outset?" The answer is that they are, within the limits of the technologies and knowledge available at the time of design. Imagine a car designed in 1961. After it is built and put on the market, two important phenomena occur. First, new materials and techniques are discovered. A 1961 car did not rely on computers, safety measures such as air-bags, lightweight-but-strong materials, and other improvements that one finds in a 1993 car. Second, the car begins to deteriorate the minute it is produced. It may age in unanticipated ways; one part may not work particularly well or could chemically alter in unforeseen ways.[4] It is only natural that advances in science and engineering should be used to improve the safety, security, and reliability of the car. Why would one not want the same principal to operate for a nuclear stockpile—on which national security depends and for which the implications of an accident are so great? It is also only natural that one would expect that improvements to a car would require testing; computer modeling would not be enough. Should one not expect the same principal of testing to be applied to weapons?

In the future, the importance of nuclear testing will become more acute because the number of nuclear weapons designs in the stockpile will decrease, as reductions in strategic nuclear weapons take effect. With fewer types of warheads, a flaw in just one design could affect a large proportion of the US nuclear forces on alert—up to 50%, depending on the design and the fault involved.

Rendering Safe

The possibility of a terrorist nuclear threat is growing. A terrorist organization—or even a proliferant country—may place a nuclear weapon in a major city and then threaten the government with its detonation. The weapon might be a primitive design, or it might be a highly sophisticated one, perhaps stolen from a nuclear weapons state's arsenal. Although either prospect has been technically possible for a long time, it is more so today. This is because of the increased amount of nuclear materials and number of states that possess weapons worldwide, and also because of the possibility of lax controls over weapons in the former Soviet Union and proliferant states.

Finding and disabling a weapon is a multistage process: there must be warning of the threat; ability to monitor key points of entry; capability to locate the weapon; methods to render it safe; and means to determine identity of the weapon's origin. Because the nuclear device might be any one of many types or designs, the tools to disable it may vary. Capabilities have been developed to disable some types of designs, but new technologies are needed for others. Computer simulation and nonnuclear testing will be extremely useful in the research and development of these technologies. Once a technology is developed to disable a terrorist weapon, however, the only sure way to know that it works is to test it. It may be possible that such testing could be conducted at a very low level of nuclear yield.

Proliferation and a Comprehensive Test Ban

Some argue that a CTB will further the cause of nuclear nonproliferation. This link is misleading for a number of reasons, including:

- Testing by declared nuclear weapon states is not a driving force behind proliferation.
- Proliferant nations do not need to test in order to acquire a first-generation nuclear weapon capability, as Pakistan and others have proven.
- The NPT does not call for a CTB. The only mention in the NPT of a CTB is in the preamble. It states that the preamble of yet another treaty (the 1963 Limited Test Ban Treaty) calls for discontinuance of all nuclear explosives testing.
- A test ban does not constitute disarmament. It does not get rid of any weapons, nor does it place any limits on further weapons production.

John Deutch, noted expert on defense and security affairs, has written,

The need for testing must be balanced against possible nonproliferation benefits of testing restraints. There are, however, several reasons to distrust linkage between testing by nuclear weapon states and the pace of proliferation. The motivation of most nations to acquire a nuclear weapon has little to do with the size or characteristics of the US arsenal. Their motivations reflect security concerns or geopolitical ambitions. These concerns will not go away if nuclear weapon states cease testing.[5]

Simple nuclear-device designs do not need to be tested. A nation can be highly confident that a simple design will work, without testing, because of the technology openly available today. If, however, the nation were to want more than a simple design, testing would probably be required. For example, if the nation were interested in developing very modern weapons, highly safe and secure weapons, or highly improved military systems to deliver nuclear warheads, testing would be needed. The bottom line is that a CTB will not present an obstacle to a nation's acquisition of nuclear weapons capability.

The notion that a CTB is required by the NPT is simply wrong. It is also untrue that additional nations would sign the NPT if there were a comprehensive ban. No countries have cited the absence of a CTB as their reason for refusing to sign a nonproliferation treaty. The reasons that countries refuse to sign or participate in nonproliferation treaties primarily have to do with their own security concerns. Pakistan won't sign the NPT until India does—and has publicly said so; India won't sign because China has nuclear weapons. It is true that India has called for a CTB. Indian officials say privately that a CTB would be valuable to prevent the further modernization of the weapons of the declared nuclear weapons states.

Few governments of NPT states view a CTB as essential to the continuation or the success of the NPT. Those officials who do link the two are often professional arms-control negotiators assigned to positions such as ambassador to the UN Conference on Disarmament in Geneva.[6] In official US government meetings with foreign representatives prior to the 1990 NPT Review Conference, some representatives in Geneva portrayed their government's position as being strongly for a CTB. In conversations directly with their government in their country's capital, however, this was frequently not the case. As one diplomat from an important NPT state noted, the issue of a CTB is just something with which to beat up on the United States.[7] He went on to say that the real issues of concern were those which directly affect the security of NPT parties, such as whether proliferant nations like Israel would join the treaty. Proliferant states are not going to test because the nuclear weapons states do. Nor are those who want to test going to refrain from doing so just because the United States or other nuclear weapons states refrain from testing.

Some proponents of a CTB are beginning to realize that the linkage with the NPT is artificial. As momentum builds for new testing limitations, perhaps even to include a CTB, supporters are seeking to dampen expectations that a CTB will bring new NPT adherents. Michael Krepon, an arms-control advocate noted for his support of a CTB, has argued that the test ban should not be linked to nonproliferation.[8]

If a nuclear test ban does not get rid of any weapons and does not have a valid link with nonproliferation, why do so many people advocate a CTB so strongly? A part of the answer is that a CTB is a symbol. As Krepon says, "The most important reason for a test ban is that it reinforces the idea that these weapons must never be used again."[9] And, there are some for whom a CTB is worthy because it is a sure way to limit the abilities of the United States to modernize and improve its nuclear forces.

Given that a CTB is an important symbol to some people, is there any reason not to go forward with it? As already discussed, one reason not to ban all testing is that improvements in safety and security of nuclear forces would no longer be possible in those states which choose to comply. More importantly, nuclear weapons states party to the ban would no longer be sure that their weapons would work, which undercuts their deterrent value. By extension, those who rely on the US or Russian nuclear deterrent would no longer be sure of its effectiveness.

The US nuclear umbrella extends over South Korea, Japan, and NATO allies. The Russian nuclear umbrella extends over Kazakhstan. If the credibility of the nuclear deterrent erodes, or if it is perceived to be degraded, as a result of no nuclear testing, some countries may believe that they would be better off with their own nuclear forces. Germany, for example, might argue that US nuclear forces are not proven dependable through regular nuclear testing. It might also think that US willingness to acquiesce to a CTB symbolizes a lack of political commitment to maintenance of the US nuclear deterrent. By this indirect means, a CTB could actually stimulate proliferation.

Despite the technical and political disadvantages of a CTB, its importance as a symbol and as a means of halting weapons improvements may be paramount to political leaderships in the United States and Russia. The United Kingdom has stated that it will not stop nuclear testing, although it currently has no test site at which to test other than in the United States. China has ignored requests that it join test limitations and continues testing. France has undertaken a moratorium, a policy which may be lifted if a conservative government were to come to power.

If a CTB is to be undertaken, there are some important questions to be resolved. There are also some important initiatives that should be considered as possible first steps.

The Verification Problem

Verification of the absence of nuclear testing, particularly at yield levels below one kiloton, is virtually impossible. Even if seismic stations were placed worldwide, there would be difficulties such as the high rate of false positives that result from natural phenomena and from chemical explosions in industry. And, to cheat, a nation would simply have to shut down the station for a limited time and say that it was out of order. Suspicions might be raised, but there would be little that could be done to prove noncompliance.

Appropriate Next Steps

North Korea, Iran, Syria, Algeria, and Iraq are some of the countries that show evidence of being interested in acquiring nuclear weapons. Libya would like to buy one or more but cannot hope to develop the requisite technology indigenously. Ukraine, Belarus, and Kazakhstan still have former-Soviet nuclear weapons. India and Israel may have sizable nuclear arsenals. Pakistan continues to make nuclear materials for weapons. China is steadily increasing the size and capabilities of its arsenal. These facts point out that both the United States and Russia are likely to need to deter nuclear forces other than each other's. And, as the nuclear arsenals of both diminish and the number of warhead designs deployed is reduced, there is increased need to be sure that the systems work—unless each country decides to rely on more "primitive" designs that would have lower reliability-testing requirements. Without testing, a large proportion of the current stockpile in either country could be rendered ineffective if just one device design were to be faulty. It would be both ironic and foolhardy for either the United States or Russia to give up nuclear testing at a time when the number of states they may have to target and deter is growing.

- The United States and Russia should develop alternative testing procedures—such as better computing capabilities and above-ground hydrodynamic testing—to help assure the workability of their arsenals.

Because the number of nuclear threats is growing, a CTB should no longer be viewed as a symbol important only to an East–West arms race. A CTB should be viewed as a worldwide requirement.

- Neither the United States nor Russia should stop all nuclear testing until all potential proliferants and existing nuclear weapons states (e.g., India, Israel, Pakistan, etc.) agree to adhere to the ban.

Implicit in the above is the fact that what is good for the United States is also good for Russia. It is in US national security interests for Russia to have high confidence that its nuclear deterrent works, so that Moscow will never be prompted to strike first out of fear that its deterrent is weak. It is also crucial to US interests that Moscow increases both the safety and security of its weapons. Russia can do neither if it has no usable test site. One of Russia's two former test sites is located in what is now Kazakhstan and the other,

Novaya Zemlya, has serious problems. Not only is it rendered virtually unusable for part of the year because of the darkness and cold (it is very far north), but it also has political problems, including opposition from the local population and nearby foreign governments.

- The United States should consider offering Russia the opportunity to utilize the Nevada Test Site to conduct tests relevant to safety, security, and reliability.

To engage the multiplicity of nuclear and near-nuclear nations in limitations or a ban on testing, there should be international negotiations. This has long been advocated by delegations at the UN Conference on Disarmament, who are skilled and prepared to take on the job. Unless all nations have the opportunity to participate in the negotiation of a ban, they may be unwilling to subscribe to the results.

- The Conference on Disarmament in Geneva is the most appropriate venue for negotiations on further testing limits or a CTB.

In the flurry of activity to develop new arms-related agreements, existing ones should not be forgotten. The 1963 Limited Test Ban Treaty limits nuclear testing to those conducted underground. Neither France nor China are party to this treaty. The 1974 Threshold Test Ban Treaty prohibits testing above 150 kilotons. Only the United States and Russia are parties.[10]

- Nuclear weapons states and potential proliferants should be encouraged to join the Limited Test Ban and Threshold Test Ban Treaties.

Conclusion

A CTB is unlikely to stop proliferation because it will do nothing to resolve the security problems which motivate nations to acquire nuclear weapons, nor will it present any technical obstacles to those nations doing so. The primary arms control effect of a CTB would be to limit or stymie the modernization programs of countries that already have nuclear weapons.

A CTB will impinge on the existing nuclear weapons states' confidence in their stockpiles and can limit their abilities to improve safety and security and to develop technologies to disable terrorist nuclear weapons. These reasons, plus the fact that verification of a CTB below 1-kiloton yields is highly unlikely, indicate that it might be prudent to continue some types and levels of testing at very low yields.

There is a strong political imperative for a CTB, as well as economic reasons for a test cessation. Such a test ban should be verifiable (i.e., apply to tests above 1 kiloton), involve all relevant nations, and should be negotiated in a multinational forum such as the Conference on Disarmament.

Notes

1. See testimony of Assistant Secretary of Energy Richard Claytor before the US Senate Foreign Relations Committee, Thursday, July 23, 1992, p. 4 (mimeo).

2. "White Paper on Nuclear Testing," February 19, 1992, contained in Testimony by Robert B. Barker, Assistant to the Secretary of Defense, before the US House of Representatives, Committee on Armed Services, Department of Energy Defense Nuclear Facilities Panel, March 31, 1992, pp. 8-9.

3. No simulation technique exists to replicate x-ray hardness testing, and an alternative is unlikely to be developed within the next 10 to 20 years.

4. There have been cases of materials changes in nuclear warheads after deployment. For example, the warhead for the Polaris submarine ballistic missile suffered corrosion that affected the performance of the warhead. This resulted in redesign and retesting.

5. John M. Deutch, "The New Nuclear Threat," *Foreign Affairs*, Fall, 1992, p. 130.

6. These assessments are based on the author's personal experiences discussing the NPT and CTB issues, as the US government official responsible for preparations for the 1990 NPT Review Conference, with representatives in foreign capitals and in Geneva and New York. Foreign capitals of less-developed countries frequently do not have the resources to spend on developing expertise within their foreign ministries on arms-control subjects and give a free hand to their ambassadors "on the scene" in Geneva and New York to develop arms-control-related policies.

7. Based on a conversation between the author, who was representing the US government, and a Middle Eastern government representative.

8. Michael Krepon, "The Road to Real Security," *The New York Times*, September 9, 1992, p. A13.

9. Ibid.

10. The republics of the former Soviet Union have agreed to abide by the treaties signed by the Soviet Union. The United Kingdom must abide by the same limitations as the United States because it conducts all of its testing in the United States.

8

Challenge Inspections

When news of the Iraqi clandestine enrichment program spread, the IAEA was widely criticized in the press. The public perceived that the regularly conducted IAEA inspections in Iraq had failed. What critics did not understand was that the IAEA inspections were not geared to finding undeclared nuclear facilities. Similarly, when it was revealed that Iraq had secretly reprocessed spent nuclear fuel to obtain less than three grams of plutonium, people questioned why the IAEA had not discovered this. Critics were right that the Iraqi action represented an attempt to begin obtaining materials for weapons. What most critics did not realize was that the amount separated was well below the threshhold for which the IAEA looks; the Iraqi plutonium did not constitute a "significant quantity."[1]

This chapter will describe IAEA safeguards inspections as they traditionally have been conceived and applied, together with a critique of why they are insufficient. It will also examine the concept of "special inspections" as well as efforts now underway to improve the ability of safeguards to detect clandestine programs like those in Iraq.

"Traditional" IAEA Safeguards Inspections

There are two basic types of IAEA safeguards, one that principally deals with non-NPT parties and another specifically addressing NPT parties. The former are referred to as INFCIRC/66 safeguards, which were drawn up in three tranches from 1964 to 1966. NPT-type safeguards, referred to as INFCIRC/153 safeguards, were completed in 1971. This chapter will focus on NPT-type, INCIRC/153 safeguards.

INFCIRC/153 safeguards were developed in accordance with Article III of the NPT. "...[T]he objective of safeguards is the timely detection of diversion of significant quantities of *nuclear material* from peaceful nuclear activities to the manufacture of nuclear weapons or of other nuclear explosive devices or for purposes unknown, and deterrence of such diversion by the risk of early detection."[2] There was an assumption that any attempts not to comply with the NPT would involve diversion of nuclear materials from peaceful nuclear programs—civil power reactors, research reactors, or other known facilities and materials, and that these peaceful activities would be declared. It was also assumed that while safeguards would detect an undeclared facility to which safeguarded nuclear material was being diverted, the states party to the NPT would bear responsibility for any efforts to detect totally autonomous undeclared nuclear facilities or fuel cycles (i.e., that made no use of diverted nuclear material).[3]

The focus on declared, peaceful activities has at least two important implications. The first is that the majority of safeguards inspections would be where the largest civil nuclear programs are located: Canada, Europe, and Japan. This made sense from the perspective that these countries possessed the greatest quantities of nuclear material. To some extent, it also reflected the prevalent worry at the time that the major proliferation risks in the post-World War II era were Japan and Germany, followed by other heavily industrialized countries. These countries were viewed as possibly having the motivation to acquire nuclear weapons, as well as the technological capability.

The second implication of the focus on declared, peaceful activities was that virtually no attention was paid to the potential of a nation developing a clandestine nuclear weapons program based on undeclared facilities. It was generally believed that nuclear facilities would be large-scale, visible, expensive operations that would be noticed. It was also believed that any nuclear weapons program attempted by a proliferant would probably be built on a civil nuclear program. This view did not take account of several factors that would develop in the late 1970s and 1980s such as the spread of know-how and technology relevant to nuclear weapons; proof that facilities using known enrichment technologies could be hidden successfully; strides in new technologies for uranium enrichment that would be easier to hide; growth of nations' indigenous technical infrastructures; and the capacity of nations to camouflage, conceal, and deceive.

Because safeguards were designed primarily to assure nondiversion of materials from declared facilities, 70% of the IAEA's inspection efforts have been in Japan, Canada, and Euratom (comprised of 12 European states, including two nuclear weapons states, France and the United Kingdom). The majority of the effort in Euratom is in Germany. Japan, Canada, and Germany, taken alone, are the subject of 56% of the IAEA's inspections. Several criticisms have been levied at this practice:

- Most inspections are in countries which are less likely to proliferate than others, like Iraq, Iran, and North Korea, whose intentions are suspect.
- The inspections are of declared facilities, whereas clandestine activities pose the more salient threat.
- Inspections in Euratom are redundant in many respects because they duplicate Euratom's own safeguards activities.

- The nuclear programs in the developed countries are so large that even reasonable quantities of materials unaccounted for (MUF) can comprise a significant quantity—enough for a bomb.

In the early 1990s, two problems galvanized the IAEA, forcing it to revamp safeguards. The first was the discovery of Iraq's clandestine nuclear weapons program. Iraq successfully violated IAEA safeguards by secretly establishing an uranium enrichment program, and irradiating and reprocessing fuel. Also, it had broken its political commitment under the NPT not to pursue nuclear weapons.

The second event was the breakup of the Soviet Union, which created a tremendous new workload for the IAEA. Not only were there fourteen new countries where there was once only one, several have significant nuclear facilities for which new safeguards arrangements must be established and inspections initiated. In the past, the Soviet Union exercised control over these facilities, requiring the return of spent fuel to Moscow's control. The same was true of fuel for some reactors in eastern Europe. Now, however, Russia is reluctant to accept the return of the fuel.

These two events occurred against a backdrop of other activity that pointed out the need for changes in IAEA practices. The IAEA was taking on new responsibilities vis-à-vis former proliferant states. The Republic of South Africa had decided to end its nuclear weapons program, join the NPT, invite the IAEA in for inspections, and place its substantial facilities and materials under safeguards. Meanwhile, Argentina and Brazil had similarly abandoned their opposition to safeguards on their indigenous nuclear activities and asked the IAEA for help in establishing inspections and safeguards. And, responding to three years of diplomatic pressures, North Korea agreed to conclude its safeguards agreement and invited inspections of any of its nuclear sites. (Subsequently, North Korea balked at a special inspection and announced its withdrawal from the NPT. This is discussed in greater detail later in this chapter.)

From the new challenges posed by these events, it was clear that the IAEA would have to change its approach to and focus on safeguards. It would not only have to find ways to save money and inspection hours so that they could be devoted to the new adherents, but it would also need to develop alternative methods and means to look for undeclared facilities.

The first problem is being addressed by revisiting solutions long under discussion, namely cutting back the level of IAEA involvement in Euratom inspections—which could save 2000 man-days and $5 to 10 million—and, perhaps, changing the tools and methodologies to inspect civil nuclear programs. For example, real-time data transmission on the status of materials is possible, although perhaps expensive. It could supplant the need for regular inspections.

These steps are controversial, however. Japanese representatives, for example, say that they are already subject to overly intensive scrutiny and that going to real-time reporting systems is unacceptable in terms of intrusion as well as cost. Other critics do not want to see changes in inspections in major industrial states because they fear that these countries are still proliferation risks and because they do not want a precedent for any safeguards responsibilites being delegated to a non-IAEA organization (viz., Euratom). If a high level of inspection activity is to be maintained in industrial states, in addition to expanded special inspections (discussed below), it will be necessary to more than double the current safeguards budget—something member states have thus far been unwilling to do.

The focus of the remainder of this chapter will be on how the IAEA is addressing the second problem, namely the need to search for undeclared facilities.

Special Inspections

INFCIRC/153 contains provision for special inspections:

(a) In order to verify the information contained in special reports; or

(b) If the Agency considers that information made available by the State, including explanations from the State and information obtained from routine inspections, is not adequate for the Agency to fulfill its responsibilities under the Agreement.[4]

Historically, the right to conduct special inspections at undeclared facilities has not been utilized. The objective of inspections—to verify quantities of materials declared—have easily been met by less adversarial, highly coordinated routine inspections involving only declared facilities.

With the Iraqi revelations, the provision in INFCIRC/153 for special inspections became the focal point of proposals to improve the IAEA's abilities to detect illicit activities. The first order of business was to obtain unanimity on the meaning and importance of special inspections. IAEA Director General Hans Blix requested that the IAEA Board of Governors reaffirm the rights of the Agency to use special inspections, which led to extensive discussions by the Board in December 1991. Some disagreements about the special inspections provision arose.

Some nations claimed that special inspections could be conducted only at facilities and locations which had been declared by the inspectee. Others emphasized the fact that consultations with the inspected state must precede any special inspection and that the state, under rules of sovereignty, could refuse. They cited the fact that Paragraph 77 of INFCIRC/153 called for consultations with the state and "As a result of such consultations the

Agency may make inspections in addition to the routine inspection effort provided for ... and may obtain access in agreement with the State to information or locations in addition to the access specified [for ad hoc and routine inspections]." If the state disagrees with the need for such special inspection, it has the right to appeal its case to the Board of Governors.

In February 1992, after extensive wrangling over wording, the Board finally approved a statement reaffirming the right of the IAEA to undertake special inspections. It was acknowledged that such inspections should occur only on rare occasions. Even though the right of special inspections has been reaffirmed, two critical questions remain:

- How will the IAEA obtain reliable information upon which to base a special inspection? and,
- Given the respect internationally for a nation's sovereignty, what will be the response of the IAEA if its request for a special inspection is refused?

The Question of Information

When it reaffirmed the right of special inspections, "The Board further reaffirmed the Agency's rights to obtain and to have access to additional information and locations in accordance with the Agency's Statute and all comprehensive safeguards agreements."[5] While this language was taken from INFCIRC/153 and therefore could not be labeled as a new power or authority for the Agency, the interpretation of this wording was new, as reflected in supplemental documents. For example, the Director General stated his intention to invite all member states to provide him with relevant information and to develop within the IAEA the capability to receive and evaluate that data.[6] This is a departure from the generally accepted past understanding that information regarding a country's nuclear activities would come only from the country in question, from IAEA activities in that country, or from data provided by a supplying country.

Some countries were upset with the idea that the Director General would solicit information (e.g., intelligence information such as that provided to the IAEA by the United States about Iraq) from third parties. The Belgian representative to the Board of Governors noted there was a danger that the Agency might act upon doubtful, arbitrary, or biased information, and that the state against which the information was directed might not have any opportunity to refute it or to justify itself.[7] Others feared that the dominant source of information would be the United States, turning the IAEA into a tool of Washington.[8] One way that the Director General sought to defuse the growing concern over the "intelligence question" was to stress that information would be sought from a variety of sources, not just from third-party intelligence agencies.

The Director General has announced plans to make use of data from press reporting and voluntary state reports on their nuclear-relevant imports and exports. (The list of equipment to be reported is essentially the same as the Nuclear Suppliers Group list of items which trigger safeguards, minus dual-use items.) It is not clear that either of these sources of information will be very useful, however. In the case of press reporting, the track record of revealing proliferant activities early is not good. An experiment was conducted by an IAEA working group to determine whether media reporting would have provided a good indication of the relevant nuclear activity in four significant cases:

- Reprocessing and previously unsafeguarded reactors in North Korea;
- Clandestine nuclear activities in Iraq;
- Uranium gaseous diffusion enrichment in Argentina; and
- Unsafeguarded enrichment activities in South Africa.

Over 2000 press reports drawn from data bases containing news reporting were screened. The press reported on these cases only when the nation in question chose to announce its activities (e.g., Argentina, North Korea, and South Africa), or when revealed to the press by officials (Iraq). The working group concluded that press reporting would not have been helpful in revealing the undeclared activities.

Likewise, the usefulness of additional import/export data in revealing undeclared activities will be limited. Most exporting nations already cooperate in supplying the IAEA with export data. Those wishing to supply nuclear-related items without controls will be aware that their sending technologies to an unsafeguarded facility may trigger unwanted attention and negative response. Importing nations will know that their transactions are being watched and will avoid open trade. Instead, they will do what Iraq did: try to manufacture indigenously as much as possible, and use subterfuge to obtain whatever is needed from abroad. The import/export reporting mechanism of the IAEA is unlikely to lessen the potential for undeclared activities; it will only reduce the likelihood that these activities will involve open importation.

Of the four information sources—inspection reports, intelligence, press coverage, and import-export data—the most likely to reveal the existence of undeclared facilities is intelligence information. Problems with IAEA use of intelligence from individual nations include:

- The issue is politically sensitive for those who fear domination of the IAEA inspections process by the United States or a group of

Western nations. Already, North Korea has denounced the IAEA for "using information and satellite data offered by a third country," accusing the IAEA of being a tool of Washington.[9]

- There is potential damage to the provider nation's sources and methods of intelligence-gathering. There will be a question of whether intelligence can be satisfactorily "sanitized" to pass to a multinational agency—one that does not have a long tradition of handling classified information—without risk of harming prospects of gathering more intelligence.[10]

- Some nations worry about the IAEA developing its own analytical capabilities to assess intelligence. It is unlikely that the IAEA could adequately train photo interpreters and other experts to analyze the incoming data, and having an assessments capability might lead eventually to intelligence gathering by the IAEA. In 1992, there was a proposal for the Director General to set up a small staff dedicated to intelligence assessments. This did not materialize, primarily because of political opposition from nations fearful that the assessments would facilitate domination of the South (less-developed countries) by the North (highly industrialized countries).

Other possibilities for diminishing dependence on national intelligence include establishing an international satellite monitoring agency (a French proposal), using commercial satellite observations as a substitute for or means of verifying national data, and in some countries, using "Open Skies" information gathering.[11] Another possibility would be for the United States, perhaps in combination with one or more other Western countries, to pool their intelligence information with Russia before presenting it to the IAEA. A formal mechanism to "multilateralize" data would lessen the chances for politicization.

The Question of Sovereignty

Over the years, the IAEA has become extremely sensitive to the issue of national sovereignty and to the fact that inspectors are essentially visitors. Inspectors go through rigorous training, a substantial portion of which deals with how to please—or at least avoid displeasing—their national hosts. Because of this "visitors' ethos," some IAEA inspectors at first had trouble dealing with the nature of the adversarial inspections in Iraq following Desert Storm and the imposition of Security Council Resolution 687. Some IAEA inspectors worried that they would not be allowed back into Iraq to conduct regular inspections if they were too aggressive in searching for undeclared activities. Some even opposed the notion of "anytime, anywhere" surprise inspections.

Although it was possible to conduct adversarial inspections in Iraq without inspectors being expelled, this case should not be extrapolated to others. Iraq had surrendered in war, and was subject to an international consensus that its weapons of mass destruction capabilities should be eliminated. To enforce this, the coalition forces against Iraq were prepared once again to do battle to assert their rights. This was proven when the coalition forces struck Iraqi nuclear-related facilities in January 1993. But, what if a country is not in the same category as Iraq?

A country that is asked to undergo a special inspection may believe that the request is based on erroneous information or is politically motivated. The nation may also be afraid that the inspection will reveal something that it wants to hide. Whatever the case, the nation has different options: it can simply deny the request and wait for the international community to try to muster the kind of consensus exercised in Iraq; it may abrogate the agreements with the IAEA,[12] and perhaps even the NPT; it can take its case to the IAEA Board of Governors and seek to undermine support for the Director General's request for a special inspection; or it can allow the inspection and, if it has something to hide, seek to make it ineffective through such means as subterfuge and deceit.

Knowing that the issue of special inspections is politically charged, the IAEA has sought to avoid them. Instead, the IAEA has worked with countries to try to obtain an invitation for any nonroutine inspection. For example, when South Africa decided to sign the NPT and subject its materials and facilities to safeguards, the IAEA wanted to visit sites that ordinarily would not be part of a facilities agreement, like the location in the Kalahari Desert long thought to be a nuclear-explosives test site.[13] An arrangement was quietly worked out whereby the IAEA would be invited by the South African government to visit the location. Similarly, Iran invited the IAEA to conduct a nonroutine visit to "suspect sites," as did North Korea.

The determination of the IAEA to make the necessary inspections, regardless of whether they are invited or by special request, has increased. In particular, North Korea's recent refusal to allow the IAEA to make a special inspection and subsequent announcement of its pullout of the NPT has raised the question of what can be done when a nation refuses to comply.

The problem of special inspections in a country that does not want to cooperate is made especially difficult by the fact that some countries are not fully committed to the concept of nuclear nonproliferation. And, any country that has something to hide can simply opt out of the safeguards system.

New Safeguards Approaches

To help countries demonstrate their good faith and compliance with the NPT, the IAEA is developing new safeguards approaches that will not have to rely on adversarial special inspections or on orchestrating invited inspections. The approaches, although not yet complete at the time of this writing, are designed to provide a means for nations to increase transparency and provide greater confidence to the international community that they are in compliance with their arms-control commitments.

Currently, the safeguards system is designed to verify the quantity of fissile materials in a given location or set of locations. These areas are referred to as Material Balance Areas (MBAs), which are defined in the operational document between the state and the IAEA, the so-called Facility Attachment. Facility Attachments specify the "strategic points" and records that the IAEA believes necessary for safeguarding declared facilities. Inspectors, therefore, have neither sought nor been granted access to facilities or locations outside of these MBAs

Following revelations of the secret nuclear program in Iraq, many states felt that a purpose of IAEA inspections should be to ascertain that no undeclared nuclear activities are being undertaken. To increase transparency and confidence, the IAEA therefore is considering new approaches which would give inspectors access to areas other than the MBAs. Various measures are being examined for increasing the transparency of a state's nuclear program, for increasing cooperation between the IAEA and a state's nuclear authorities, for enhancing the IAEA's inspection capability to detect undeclared nuclear activities, and for facilitating and expediting inspections at undeclared sites. These inspections would differ not only in their broader access but also in their nonscheduled nature. Some might be conducted with due cause, others just to maintain the credibility of the approach.

Transparency might be enhanced by the state's regular provision of reports on its activities—reports that go beyond the accounting information now submitted. For example, the state might report on facility operations so as to enable the IAEA to better select the timing of a visit.

An incentive for a state to participate in the new safeguards approaches— aside from promoting others' confidence in its compliance record—is a reduced number of routine inspections. This is very important to many states that believe their nuclear programs encounter significant costs and delays as a result of routine inspections as currently conducted. Routine inspections would not be diminished on sensitive parts of the nuclear fuel cycle where highly enriched uranium or separated plutonium might be produced, stored, or used.

Facilities capable of separating plutonium, handling separated plutonium, or enriching uranium present the greatest challenges to any safeguards inspections—traditional, modified, special, or invited. Because
plutonium or enriched uranium is required for nuclear explosives, they
constitute the most important activity to control. To have confidence that
a given nation is not secretly developing nuclear explosives, there should be
a way to determine that a nation has no clandestine reprocessing or
enrichment activities.

Secret enrichment activities would be very hard, if not impossible to
discover if a capable nation were intent on hiding them.[14] Some enrichment
technologies would be more difficult to discover than others. Isotope
separation via lasers or chemical processes, for example, can take only a
small amount of space and energy and can be controlled to minimize
detectable emissions. Large, energy-consuming gaseous diffusion plants
are more observable. Iraq proved, however, that some technologies ordinarily considered "visible" can be hidden. It successfully built and operated
portions of a secret large-scale, high-energy-intensive enrichment plant
(using electromagnetic isotope separation technology). This operation was
not detected by US intelligence.

Reprocessing activities are harder to hide. A reprocessing facility must
have very thick concrete walls because of the intense radioactivity of the
materials. If built above ground or in the open, this might be observable.
More importantly, however, reprocessing emissions are distinctive and can
be detected several kilometers away. While it may be technically possible
to build such a facility underground and to mask emissions, it would be
extremely difficult and expensive. If, however, the facility were located in
or near a plant where legitimate, declared, safeguarded reprocessing ordinarily takes place, it probably would be impossible to distinguish emissions
from the clandestine, illicit activity.

The new approaches to safeguards being considered by the IAEA would
be voluntary. Additionally, the IAEA has sought to strengthen the safeguards regime that all NPT parties are now obliged to accept. These
measures include the right to special inspections, as mentioned above.
Additionally, the IAEA Board of Governors has decided that all states
should provide early, full information about new facilities and any modifications to existing facilities. The Board has also called for more comprehensive reporting of exports. These measures apply to all states and are
independent of any new safeguards approaches.

Conclusion

Safeguards inspections in the past have not been designed to detect
undeclared nuclear facilities or activities. Now that it is clear from the case

of Iraq that such activities are possible—even in an NPT party that subjects itself to safeguards—the IAEA is seeking to find new ways to lessen the likelihood of undeclared activities going undetected. New approaches being examined would provide for new IAEA inspection measures for detecting undeclared nuclear facilities, would increase the amount of voluntary reporting by a nation, and would allow inspectors to visit any sites, without regard to whether or not they have been declared and are under safeguards. This is a positive step because it will increase somewhat the confidence that the nation in question is in compliance. Problems that cannot be overcome even by these reforms in safeguards inspections include:

- There are no high-confidence technologies to locate secret enrichment facilities or detect, from a long range, clandestine enrichment activities. Nor are there technologies that can detect secret reprocessing activities under some conditions.
- Inspections will continue to be voluntary, with the exception of extreme cases such as Iraq.
- The necessity of depending on some nations' intelligence reporting will be politically unpalatable to many countries.

Notes

1. "Significant quantity" is a term used to denote the amount of plutonium or enriched uranium needed to make a nuclear explosive, 8 and 25 kilograms respectively.

2. International Atomic Energy Agency, INFCIRC/153 (Corrected), *The Structure and Content of Agreements Between The Agency and States Required in Connection with the Treaty on the Nonproliferation of Nuclear Weapons,* (IAEA: Vienna, 1972), paragraph 28.

3. David Fischer and Paul Szasz, "The Risk of Secret Nuclear Plants," *Safeguarding the Atom, A Critical Appraisal* (London and Philadelphia: Taylor and Francis, 1985), pp. 36–37.

4. IAEA, INFCIRC/153, paragraph 73.

5. IAEA Board of Governors, "Record of the Seven Hundred and Seventy-Sixth Meeting," GOV/OR.776, April 9, 1992, p. 16.

6. IAEA document GOV/2554, Attachment 1.

7. IAEA, GOV/OR.776, p. 17.

8. In confidential interviews by the author with thirteen IAEA officials in November 1992, six noted that the Agency's reliance on the United States for intelligence would be a serious problem, particularly if it became evident that special inspections resulted from Washington's instigation.

9. David E. Sanger, "Reversing Its Earlier Stance, North Korea Bars Nuclear Inspectors," *The New York Times, International,* February 9, 1993, p. A2.

10. The IAEA is a multilateral institution staffed by experts of many nationalities. Sometimes information that should be treated as confidential is passed by staff members to their respective governments.

11. David Fischer, private communication to the author, March 1993.

12. The IAEA does not recognize the right of a nation to abrogate its safeguards agreement. The only legal way to terminate an NPT safeguards agreement is to withdraw from the NPT. In that case, any suspended safeguards agreements would reenter into force. Despite legalities, however, the nation with safeguarded facilities could just refuse to participate in safeguards inspections and be willing to take whatever political or military repercussions there might be.

13. Interview by the author with officials in Vienna, Austria IAEA Headquarters in November, 1992.

14. This refers to detection of the activity by national technical means. The activity could readily be detected were there to be accurate information provided by a human source.

9

International Sanctions

In discussions of how to handle proliferation, often the argument for sanctions and reprisals is made. Usually, the type of sanctions advocated is economic, although political and military are also options. Economic sanctions are intended to cost the offending nation so much financially, that a cost-benefit analysis will lead that nation to abandon whatever it is doing that sparked the sanctions. An example is the United Nations embargo of Iraq. Military sanctions deprive the country in question of the hardware, advice, training, or other assistance that it would ordinarily expect to receive. United States assistance to Pakistan's military was curtailed as a result of its nuclear proliferation. Political sanctions consist of efforts to deprive the nation of full participation in the international political system. South Africa was target of UN political sanctions, which resulted in South Africans being barred from a variety of functions, including participation in international sports events.

How successful are sanctions in accomplishing their goal? More specifically, how likely are they to prevent or reverse proliferation? The remainder of this chapter will address these two questions.

Are Sanctions Successful?

Sanctions are designed to influence a target nation to undertake or to desist an action, policy, or behavior. They may be effected by one nation against another, or by a multinational group such as the United Nations. Sanctions are considered effective if they accomplish their stated goal, within the time frame specified. The principal variables that determine whether sanctions are effective in accomplishing their goal are outlined in Table 3.

The first determinant is the relative reliance of the offending country on the commodity of which it is being deprived under the sanctions. Some countries may be highly self-sufficient, not relying on outside aid or on imports. Economically, they may be able to sustain sanctions, even if they result in loss of standard-of-living for the general population. Sanctions against Iraq before and after Desert Storm caused significant economic hardship for the population, but they were endured without much domes-

TABLE 3 Determinants of Successful Sanctions

- Reliance of the targeted country on the commodity of which it is being deprived.

- Degree to which the nation(s) applying sanctions is a provider of desired or required commodities.

- Availability of alternative sources for the commodity.

- Ability of the targeted nation to retaliate, making the cost of sanctions not worth the benefit.

- Degree of commitment by the nation(s) employing sanctions.

tic protest for many reasons, including the highly repressive nature of the Saddam Hussein regime, which muted opposition.

The degree of repressiveness of the regime and its ability to force its people to withstand significant hardship can lessen the impact that sanctions have on a country's behavior. Or, the impact of sanctions may be tempered by popular indignation; the target country's people may rally against the sanctions and work to negate or ignore the ill effects.

Politically, a nation may be aloof or isolated, not caring much what others think of its policies or behavior. North Korea is such a country, not placing particularly high value on whether the international community approves of its actions. Effecting political sanctions against North Korea to limit or bar its role in international relations would be unlikely to achieve the goal of the sanctions. In fact, political sanctions could even be counterproductive, making the nation feel justified in its rejection of international norms and requirements.

A second determinant of sanctions' effectiveness is whether the country or countries engaged in applying sanctions are the providers of the commodity. If the United States cuts off economic assistance to a country as a sanction, but in reality provides only a small fraction of the offending nation's supply of foreign assistance, it will not be likely to matter much.

Closely related to the above is the question of whether there are alternative suppliers of the embargoed items—a third determinant of the effectiveness of sanctions. There have been numerous instances when the United States and others have cut off the supply of armaments to a given country as sanctions. Very often, these sanctions are easily circumvented. Armaments are often plentiful on the black market, or there are other countries willing to fill the gap.

The effectiveness of sanctions may be diluted by a fourth factor, the ability of the targeted nation to retaliate and levy unacceptable damage on the country undertaking sanctions. For example, countries dependent on imported oil have always been reluctant to engage in punitive sanctions against Arab oil suppliers for fear that their economic lifeblood of energy supplies would be cut off. There are also political means of retaliation. Iraq announced that it would not free two arrested Britons until the United Kingdom released frozen Iraqi assets.[1] The United Kingdom froze them in an attempt to force Iraqi compliance with post-Desert Storm resolutions. Although only two hostages are unlikely to force a change in London's policy, a significant number of hostages held for a long time can be used to force an end to sanctions. Iran used the US hostages it held to obtain concessions from Washington, including a secret deal to break a ban on arms sales to Iran.

Occasionally, conscious retaliation by the targeted country is not undertaken, but the effects of sanctions nevertheless cause unacceptable damage to the nation applying sanctions. In 1987, the United States initiated sanctions against Haiti to compel the government to allow a freely elected civilian government, respect human rights, and cease drug-smuggling activities. The sanctions had serious effects and were partly responsible for causing large numbers of refugees to flee by boat to the United States. The influx of economic refugees was so great that the United States was forced to spend large sums intercepting, housing, and processing the Haitians. The sanctions were eased in 1990, and none of the objectives were met. Washington is fearful of reinstating sanctions because of the effect it is likely to have on illegal immigration to the United States.

A fifth determinant is the degree of participation in the sanctions. All or most of the countries able to supply significant quantities of the commodity must participate. And, the participation must be more than nominal. Often, nations have superficially participated in sanctions, but have actually become surreptitious suppliers, usually motivated by economic gain.

In the past, sanctions usually have failed to accomplish their stated aim because of problems with one or more of the determinants (see Table 2). As the political scientist Klaus Knorr noted, "[C]oercively wielding economic power by means of trade reprisals or special trade advantages is rarely successful, because even states of great economic strength do not command a compelling degree of monopolistic or monopsonistic control in their foreign trade, and because the punishment that can be imposed by these means does not inflict enough pain, on the one hand, and tends to arouse the will to resist, on the other. This is not to say, of course, that no power whatever inheres in this sort of commercial strength. There is just ordinarily not very much. Occasionally, some special combination of circumstances is apt to make it an important weapon."[2]

There are several excellent reviews of sanctions that demonstrate their very limited success.[3] A 1990 study of 115 international trade embargoes against various countries made by the Washington-based Institute for International Economics concluded that only a minority had achieved their political goals and that the percentage of success was declining as targeted nations grow more sophisticated at evading blockades.[4] Some examples of current sanctions cases are listed below, along with the reasons for their failure or success.

   1. United Nations versus Yugoslavia, May 1992[5]
      Objective: Use trade sanctions against Serbia and Montenegro to halt Serbian aggression. All strategic materials such as gasoline, tires, aircraft, and chemicals are banned to cripple Serbia's capability to wage war.
      Effectiveness: Failure. Arms and petroleum products slipped through with ease. The United Nations acknowledged the ineffectiveness, enacting a naval blockage in November 1992.
   2. United Nations versus Libya[6]
      Objective: To force surrender of Libyan intelligence officers suspected of masterminding the bombing of Pan Am Flight 103 over Scotland, on December 21, 1988. Sanctions included a ban on air travel and weapons-related sales to Libya.
      Effectiveness: Failure. To date, the men have not surrendered or been handed over by Libyan authorities. Libya has circumvented export controls. For example, it has obtained equipment for a second chemical weapons plant by importing from Germany, Switzerland, Britain, and Japan—routing some items through Singapore to evade detection.[7]
   3. Western governments (minus Japan) versus China[8]
      Objective: Export restrictions and financial sanctions were imposed to punish Chinese leaders for the Tiananmen Square Massacre in June, 1989. The goal was to force China to improve its human rights policies and practice of democracy.
      Effectiveness: Failure. China continued with persecution of students and with executions. The United States diluted its participation in the sanctions by renewing most-favored-nation trading status for China in May 1990. China's large foreign cash reserves make it less susceptible to economic sanctions.

Perhaps the best example of the problems associated with international sanctions is the case of UN sanctions against Iraq. Iraq would seem to be an ideal candidate for effective sanctions. It violated international law, resulting in a unusual UN consensus. The prospects for full-scale international participation in the sanctions were therefore high. Iraq obtained 98% of its foreign exchange from oil. Thus, disallowing oil sales would be expected to have tremendous economic impact. And, the country's economy was severely stressed by the effects of Operation Desert Storm. Despite these "favorable" conditions, sanctions have not been very effective. For example, they have not resulted in achieving the objective of inducing Saddam Hussein's cooperation with UN efforts to eliminate Iraq's weapons of mass destruction and missiles. In fact, Iraq has fared well, as the following quotation from journalist Paul Lewis shows.

> *Two years after a strict embargo was imposed on Iraq, the country has repaired almost all the 134 bridges cut by allied bombing, rebuilt hundreds of miles of damaged road and railway track, and restored ravaged electrical grids, communications networks and broadcast equipment. Just how Iraq has succeeded in repairing all this damage while bound by an import embargo and under intermittent threat of attack is a closely guarded secret. But experts assume a combination of sanctions busting, improvisation and domestic manufacture of needed parts has allowed Mr. Hussein to stabilize Iraq's economy at a low but sustainable level of activity, making outright collapse unlikely.[9]*

These are but a few of the many cases in which sanctions have been levied in an attempt to compel a specific nation to undertake or refrain from an action or behavior. While none of these examples show sanctions to be very effective, they can be if conditions—based on the determinants in Table 2— are favorable. The subject nation must be vulnerable, the sanctions tight, and alternative suppliers must refrain from filling the gap. Also, the sanctions must not present an unacceptable burden to the nation(s) effecting the sanctions.

One example of a case in which these conditions were met was in the sanctions levied against the Ugandan government of Idi Amin between 1972 and 1979. Sanctions by the United States and United Kingdom were designed to foment unrest against Amin. Sanctions worked well with other forces—such as military pressures by neighboring Tanzania—to bring Amin down.

Can Sanctions Prevent or Reverse Proliferation?

These examples show that the effectiveness of sanctions depend on the circumstances of a given situation. The first question is whether the proliferant is vulnerable. Does it rely on the commodity of which it will be deprived under sanctions? If the sanctions are economic, the proliferant nation is unlikely to be very susceptible.

Nuclear proliferation—assuming it is indigenous production of a weapon rather than theft—is extraordinarily expensive. Producing special nuclear materials can cost hundreds of millions of dollars. Developing high explosives, delivery systems, and other aspects of the program will drive the price into the billions of dollars. So, the nation is already sacrificing economically. It is forgoing economic development and private-sector growth for the sake of its weapons program. Compared to such a sacrifice, the loss of trade or economic assistance from the nations applying sanctions is unlikely to matter greatly.

It may be that the proliferant country is not very reliant on international trade or assistance in the first place. In the past, some nuclear proliferants have been pariahs in the international community. South Africa was already under heavy sanctions in order to punish its policy of Apartheid when it was working on nuclear weapons. Taiwan was highly self-reliant economically when it started its weapons program in the 1970s (later abandoned because of political pressures and promises from Washington). North Korea is the nation-state equivalent of a recluse, as it pursues nuclear weapons technology. Israel was isolated and at war with others in the Middle East as it developed its capabilities. These nations were seeking nuclear weapons, in part, for the very reasons that they were internationally rejected and felt threatened. This feature of rejection by others makes them less subject to application of international sanctions. To have the threat of being made a pariah made meaningful, the nation must not already be a pariah.

Another reason that sanctions may not work vis-à-vis nuclear proliferants is the availability of alternative sources for whatever is being denied. In the case of economic punishment, usually the only assistance cut off is nonhumanitarian. Food and other aid continues to flow. It is merely a matter of budget shuffling to move a state's monies for civil programs into the military sector (to pay for nuclear weapons) and use foreign aid to pay for the civil programs. In the case of military-related sanctions, spare parts and weaponry are often available on the black market or from a multiplicity of sources.

Proliferant nations may also deter or undermine sanctions by presenting the sanctioning country(ies) with unacceptable costs. Pakistan provides an excellent example. The United States cut off economic aid to Pakistan in 1977 because it was trying to import reprocessing technology from France, which was totally unjustifiable for a civil program and was apparently for weapons development. Pakistan did not alter its behavior in the nuclear arena, but the United States shut off the deal by pressuring France. Aid to Pakistan was restored in 1978, without Pakistan changing its intentions. As Pakistani efforts to obtain weapons-related technologies continued, the United States again cut off aid in 1979. Six months later, the United States resumed aid—not because Pakistan changed, but because Washington was encountering an unacceptable cost for its sanctions. Pakistan would not cooperate with Washington's campaign to assist the rebels fighting the Soviet Union in Afghanistan unless the sanctions were removed.

Conclusion

Nations pursuing nuclear weapons capability ordinarily do so because they believe that possession will deter or counter a perceived threat. In some cases, the motivation may be prestige or aggression. In any case, the threat posed by potential sanctions would have to have greater value to the proliferant than fulfilling the objective of weapons acquisition. In the case of most proliferant states, this would mean that the threat of sanctions would have to be more serious than the national security threat that the weapons are intended to counter.

Notes

1. "Iraq Says It Won't Free 2 Britons Till London Releases Assets," *The New York Times International*, February 11, 1993, p. A4.

2. Klaus Knorr, *The Power of Nations: The Political Economy of International Relations* (New York: Basic Books, 1975), p. 165.

3. In addition to Klaus Knorr's work, cited above, see Robin Renwick, *Economic Sanctions* (Cambridge: Harvard University, 1981), and Barry E. Carter, *International Economic Sanctions: Improving the Haphazard US Legal Regime* (Cambridge: Cambridge University Press, 1988).

4. Clyde Hufbauer, Jeffrey J. Schott, and Kimberly Ann Elliott, *Economic Sanctions Reconsidered: History and Current Policy*, Second Edition, Volumes 1 & 2 (Washington, DC: Institute for International Economics, 1990).

5. Frank J. Prial, "UN Tightens Curbs on Belgrade By Authorizing a Naval Blockade," *The New York Times*, November 17, 1992, p. A1, and William Drozdiak, "NATO Agrees to Impose Blockade of Serbia," *The Washington Post*, November 19, 1992, p. A31.

6. George Lardner, Jr., "Clinton Is Reminded of Pledge To Press For Libyan Oil Embargo," *The Washington Post*, November 17, 1992, p. A4.

7. R. Jeffrey Smith, "Libya's New Poison Gas Effort Assailed," *The Washington Post*, February 19, 1993, p. A27.

8. Hufbauer, Schott, and Elliott, Volume 1, pp. 268-282.

9. Paul Lewis, "Hussein Rebuilds Iraq's Economy Undeterred by the UN Sanctions," *The New York Times*, January 24, 1993, p. A1.

10

Security Assurances

The principal reason that nations want to acquire nuclear weapons is for security. They perceive some threat—whether nuclear, chemical, biological, or conventional—that they believe will be best handled by having a nuclear deterrent. In the past, nations have also been motivated by desire for prestige, but today this plays a lesser role given the high political cost of weapons possession. Additionally, force projection has also been a motive. Saddam Hussein, for example, not only sought nuclear weapons partly to counter Israel's nuclear arsenal but also to support its hegemonistic advances toward Kuwait, Iran, and others. Security assurances can do little to dampen the motivations for prestige or force projection, but they can be very effective in lessening the security concerns that may foster nuclear proliferation.

Security assurances may either be negative or positive. The former is a promise by a nuclear weapons possessor not to use those weapons to threaten or attack a nonpossessor. (The specific terms of the assurance may vary, as explained in Chapter 1.) Positive assurances are a pledge to come to a particular nonpossessor's assistance in the event that it is threatened. Both types of security assurances have played roles in preventing nuclear proliferation in the past, but the success of positive assurances is somewhat easier to discern.

Positive Security Assurances

The North Atlantic Treaty Organization (NATO) and the Warsaw Pact were extremely influential in forestalling nuclear proliferation in Europe following World War II. Through NATO, the United States provided a nuclear deterrent to Western Europe vis-à-vis the Soviet Union and Warsaw Pact states. The deterrent was a promise by the superpowers to their pact members to use their nuclear arsenals, if necessary, to respond to either a nuclear or overwhelming conventional attack/threat. During the height of the Cold War, tactical nuclear weapons were placed on European soil by both the United States and Soviet Union to reassure their respective clients that the deterrent they were providing was real and immediate.

Both pacts served to delegitimize any aspirations for nuclear weapons by non-nuclear-weapons member states. Furthermore, the NATO pact lessened the propensity for the United Kingdom and France—both of whom had nuclear weapons—to develop large, diversified nuclear arsenals.

In addition to undermining the reasons a pact member might have for wanting nuclear weapons, the security agreements enabled a check on "adventurism." Any unilateral efforts by a pact member, east or west, almost certainly would have been detected, given the close association of the militaries of the respective member states. Each superpower would have been in a position to exert tremendous pressure on any potential proliferant within its pact.

Although NATO and the Warsaw Pact functioned as nuclear nonproliferation tools, they were not designed primarily as such. Their primary mission, initially, was to stabilize the political boundaries of Europe following World War II and to forestall a conventional rearming on the continent. There are cases, however, in which positive security assurances have played an explicit role in deterring nuclear proliferation. South Korea is such a case.

In the mid-1970s, the Cold War was still going strong; its impact was especially felt in the East–West conflict transposed onto North and South Korea. South Korea felt vulnerable, particularly to any attack by North Korea in which support might be provided from a nuclear weapons state— the Soviet Union or China. South Korea's military rulers decided to tap the country's tremendous technical expertise in its civil nuclear power industry to make nuclear weapons.

The United States learned of the South Korean nuclear weapons program and sought to discourage it. Given that South Korea felt its vital security interests were at stake, it was not willing to give up the option unless the United States reaffirmed its extension of a nuclear umbrella over South Korea and reversed President Carter's decision to withdraw 25% of US forces stationed in South Korea. The US government calculated that it was worthwhile to meet South Korea's security requirements in return for a South Korean agreement not to develop nuclear weapons.

North Korea feared and resented the US positive security assurances to South Korea. It continually insisted that any tactical nuclear weapons stationed in South Korea be removed, and began secretly trying to develop its own nuclear weapons capability.

North Korea's failure to sign a safeguards agreement on its nuclear facilities—as required by the NPT, which had been signed by North Korea in 1985—fed international suspicions that illicit nuclear activities might be underway. North Korea agreed to invite the IAEA for a visit to its nuclear facilities and to discuss confidence-building measures with South Korea, but only if certain conditions were met. The primary requirement was that

US nuclear weapons be removed from South Korea. In late 1991, the United States assured that there were no nuclear weapons in South Korea. US reaffirmed its commitment to the defense of South Korea. Not only will US forces remain, but also US strategic nuclear weapons could be used to maintain the umbrella, as needed.

"In January 1992, North Korea signed a declaration with South Korea on the denuclearization of the Korean Peninsula. Both parties agreed not to manufacture or receive nuclear weapons and not to build plutonium separation or enrichment plants."[1] Four months later, North Korea concluded a safeguards agreement and allowed IAEA inspections.

In conjunction with the withdrawal of nuclear weapons from the peninsula, the United States reaffirmed its security assurance to South Korea and agreed to conduct joint military exercises in 1993, despite strong North Korean denunciations. Other nations represented in the IAEA also were critical of the exercises, believing it to be more important to keep dialog with North Korea going than to provide a symbol of commitment to South Korea. From another viewpoint, however, conducting the joint exercises can be seen as an integral part of the US security assurance, which is the primary factor in inhibiting nuclear proliferation in South Korea.

Meanwhile, the IAEA inspection revealed disturbing results: indications that North Korea reprocessed more plutonium than it had admitted, and on more occasions. This led to an IAEA request for a special inspection.[2] In response, North Korea announced its intent to withdraw from the NPT on March 12, 1993, citing as its reasons the threat posed by US–South Korea joint exercises and the IAEA reliance on US intelligence regarding North Korean nuclear facilities. North Korea claimed that the IAEA had become a tool of the United States.

Another instance in which the United States used security assurances to try to prevent nuclear proliferation is the case of Taiwan, about which very little is publicly known. Reportedly, Taiwan undertook a nuclear weapons program in the late 1970s.[3] United States pressures to stop the program were intense and Taiwan, a nation that is technically and financially capable of developing nuclear weapons, apparently did not proceed with its weapons program. The United States support of Taiwan's defense has been steadily maintained, despite strong tilting toward China, particularly during the four years of President Bush's administration.

Security assurances involving nuclear weapons have clearly played a role in helping to prevent nuclear proliferation. In cases where the potential proliferant perceives that it is threatened by nuclear weapons of an enemy, any promises of security assurances not involving a nuclear umbrella are unlikely to be convincing or effective. Nevertheless, there are serious obstacles to using nuclear security assurances in the future.

Problems with Nuclear Security Assurances

Since the 1970s, political and emotional opposition to nuclear weapons—as well as nuclear energy—has grown profoundly. There is strong public reaction against even the word *nuclear*. For example, a technique used by medical doctors to examine intrabody tissues was once called "magnetic nuclear resonance." Adverse public reaction led to renaming the process, "magnetic resonance imaging." The disaster at Chernobyl and facts about the tremendous environmental damage at nuclear production sites in the United States and former Soviet Union have compounded public fears. In terms of nuclear weapons, however, public rejection is particularly strong. In the United States, public support for any new role for nuclear weapons is unlikely to be high.

In the past, nuclear security assurances were more acceptable to the US public because they were made primarily as an extension existing of conventional military commitments. The two prominent past instances in which the United States provided such assurances—Europe and South Korea—involved countries where US forces had fought wars and had a deep stake in the security of those nations. In the near future, similar circumstances are unlikely to prevail.

The reticence to provide US nuclear security assurances is likely to grow, in part, because of the proliferation of technologies that would allow nations to retaliate directly against United States' territory. Imagine a hypothetical scenario. The United States convinces Pakistan to give up nuclear weapons in return for a US nuclear umbrella. India continues building its nuclear arsenal, and succeeds in developing an intercontinental ballistic missile. A ground attack is launched by India against Pakistan, and the latter appeals to the United States to muster all of its resources, including nuclear, to defend Pakistan. Pakistan would be justified in such an appeal because it had forsworn nuclear weapons—which might have defended it against an overwhelming conventional attack—only upon US security assurances.

In such a scenario, the United States would be faced with a number of problems, including the fact that it would want to avoid nuclearizing a conventional conflict. Also, in using nuclear weapons, the United States might prompt India to launch a nuclear attack against US territory.

There would be a host of other questions. For example, would it have been possible that Pakistan stimulated the attack by India, feeling secure under the US nuclear umbrella? The US military would not have the same level of integration and influence in Pakistan that it has vis-à-vis NATO countries or South Korea so it would not be in a position to adequately assess where blame should lie or prevent conflict before it erupts. Overall, a nuclear security assurance to a country other than a very close ally could result in instabilities rather than promoting peace.

Some of the concerns noted in the hypothetical scenario above have been expressed in the case of Ukraine, a former Soviet republic which has sought security assurances from the United States. Ukrainian leaders have suggested that they would not be willing to give up former-Soviet nuclear weapons now stationed on their soil unless several conditions are met, one of which is security assurances vis-à-vis Russia, a country which will retain nuclear weapons. (This subject is explored in detail in Chapter 4.) Specifics of the Ukraine request are unclear; various reports have said that Ukraine wants to join NATO, or that it simply wishes to have the US nuclear umbrella in event of a nuclear threat or attack from Russia.

To date, the United States has been unwilling to provide security assurances to Ukraine, partly to avoid sending a political signal of mistrust to Moscow. But some of the questions noted above in the hypothetical scenario also apply. A principal question is: Would the United States want to risk all-out nuclear exchange with Russia because of a commitment to Ukraine to protect it from Russian attack, particularly a conventional attack? Most in the US public and government would probably respond, no. If the probability is high that security assurances will lead to a nuclear exchange, then the US desire to make such assurances is likely to be low.

Thus far, this discussion has focused on reasons why a nuclear weapons state such as the United States would not be likely to want to offer nuclear security assurances in return for nuclear nonproliferation, despite having done so in the past. From the perspective of the potential proliferant, there are also problems with accepting and believing in nuclear security assurances. A central concern of any recipient of such assurances is whether the provider has the will and the ability to follow through.

Evaluating the *will* of the United States to fulfill its security commitments is a subjective process; evaluating *ability* is more concrete. The ability of the United States to extend a nuclear umbrella is a function of the number of reliable nuclear weapons it has. If there are enough weapons to fulfill the missions of US security and commitments to present allies—and all of the weapons are perceived to be in working order—then there should be no technical problem with the ability to provide a nuclear deterrent.

In the near future, there may be reason to question the ability of the United States to provide a nuclear deterrent on behalf of others. START and post-START arms reductions will lower the US nuclear stockpile to about 3000 weapons. If, in the future, even lower levels are agreed, the tasks which the stockpile can perform become more limited. That is, they can be used to counter the Russian nuclear arsenal, but little else. Any retargeting of US weapons when the stockpile is low would result in significantly greater advantage by the Russian arsenal.

Even more important than the question of numbers is the issue of reliability. After the currently planned reductions, there will be only five warhead designs in the US stockpile. If a flaw were found with just one warhead design, as much as 50% of the US nuclear forces on alert could be rendered unreliable. This would stretch the credibility of the US arsenal vis-à-vis Russia, let alone another country such as a potential proliferant's adversary.

Another issue is nuclear testing. US nuclear weapons designers have always stated that they need nuclear testing to determine if designs in the stockpile are continuing to work as planned. The majority of the members in the US Congress have not found that argument convincing, have cut funding for testing, and have stated support for ending testing altogether. This is a political and financial decision, not a technical or national security one. Thus, the question is: Will the nation depending on the US nuclear deterrent believe the politicians or the actual designers of the weapons?

The above discussion focused on the idea of a nation providing nuclear security assurances. Some analysts have also stated that an international nuclear force is credible and should be considered.[4] The idea is that nuclear weapons would be given up by any nation that possess them and put under the control of an international body, perhaps the United Nations. These weapons would be used to give all nations positive security assurances.

An internationalized nuclear force has many problems that make the idea untenable. There are practical issues such as how the weapons will be cared for; by whom; where they will be located; how they will be kept safe and secure; and how weapons data will be kept from possible proliferants or terrorists. These are troublesome issues for the nations giving up weapons as well as those that would be protected by them. Current weapons states will be giving up a certain deterrent for an uncertain one; it is like trading a weapon in the hand for a defender with the weapon in his hand. Will that defender act in an effective manner exactly at the time needed? Will the defender be viewed as credible by potential enemies? Non-nuclear-weapons states probably will not have any more confidence in the protective power of an international nuclear force than they do in the current UN peacekeeping forces. Such international efforts not only depend on getting political concensus—often either time consuming or impossible to reach—but also keeping it. If the United Nations Security Council, consisting of only a few nations, cannot reach a conclusion on taking nonmilitary action against North Korea for its violation of the Nuclear Nonproliferation Treaty, how can the body be expected to decide on using or threatening to use nuclear weapons against a nation?

A variation on the idea of an international nuclear force is for two or more nuclear weapons states to join forces in offering security assurances. For example, the United States and Russia together might offer positive security assurances to India and Pakistan as part of a no-nuclear-weapons zone in

South Asia. Such a proposal would have some problems discussed above, but it would be far more workable than a UN-type arrangement.

Problems with Conventional Security Assurances

The dazzling array of high-precision, devastating conventional weaponry displayed in Desert Storm provided future aggressors with a glimpse of what they may face. These weapons raise the prospect that an effective deterrent against an enemy armed with weapons of mass destruction need not be nuclear. Could a potential proliferant be convinced to give up a nuclear weapons option in return for a conventional, positive security assurance from the United States? The first problem with a "conventional umbrella" is expense. Take for example the single 1993 US attack against an Iraqi machine-tools plant associated with that country's nuclear program. Forty Tomahawk cruise missiles, at a cost of $1 million each, were launched at the facility, damaging but not destroying it. The $40 million cost of the attack probably exceeded the value of the damage caused. In the case of Desert Storm, the goal of ousting Iraq from Kuwait was accomplished but at an exceedingly high financial cost—over $61 billion, of which allied commitments financed $54 billion.[5] Because oil-rich countries like Kuwait and Saudi Arabia and oil-dependent countries like Japan were willing to help pay, the economic burden of the war was shared. For one nation or even a few to bear the cost of a conventional defense on behalf of another— particularly when use of high-technology weapons is anticipated—is likely to be too costly to make the practice common.

A second problem is credibility of the conventional deterrent, which is particularly pertinent when the threatened country is confronted by weapons of mass destruction—nuclear, chemical, or biological. The aggressor could issue a threat along the following lines: "Give me what I want or I will eliminate the population of your capital. And don't try to scare me with the conventional might of the United States behind you. Trying to use conventional means to fight me will take days, weeks, or months, and I can deliver my weapon of mass destruction against your capital within hours. You may convince the United States to undertake conventional reprisal against me, but you will already be devastated. Furthermore, I will turn my weapons of mass destruction loose on any US troops that muster to fight their conventional war. I guarantee you, Washington will cower at the thought."

Although Washington might not cower, it would pause, just as it did when Saddam Hussein's chemical weapons were considered. There already were tremendous fears of extensive battle casualties to be endured in a conventional conflict. Additionally, some members of Congress, press commentators, and others cited their fear of Iraq's chemical weapons as a reason for opposing the war. Had Iraq possessed nuclear weapons, it is doubtful that the United States would have participated in Desert Storm for fear that it could lead to nuclear weapons use.

Nuclear weapons are more powerful and terrible than conventional weaponry, but this imbalance is not the only problem with using the latter to deter the former. There is also the problem of logistics and timeliness of answering a threat. It should not be forgotten that before Desert Storm, there was Desert Shield, the five-month process of transporting troops, weaponry, and supplies to the region. Such a buildup would be required for any conventional deterrent to have credibility. Additionally, airstrips and other support facilities would be necessary in the country or region in need of defense.

Defenses

A measure is needed that reassures countries but does not incure high costs, raise the risk of nuclear exchange, or create other disadvantages associated with positive and negative security assurances. One possible answer is defenses, particularly those which will minimize the chances of delivering a nuclear weapon.

Nations that want nuclear weapons to deter a nuclear adversary are usually more worried about the prospect of a nuclear attack via aircraft or missile than about clandestine delivery of a single weapon. If the possibility of a *successful* air attack can be significantly lowered, the threat posed by that nuclear adversary is diminished—perhaps to the point where the nation's own nuclear proliferation will be viewed as unnecessary. It is imperative, however, that there be high confidence that the adversary's delivery systems will be intercepted and destroyed.

Prior to the 1980s, capable defenses against ballistic-missile delivery systems were not feasible. With the advent of "Star Wars" research by the United States, the concept became technically credible, but highly controversial. Not only was it viewed as expensive, but also was attacked by the Soviet Union as being a path to the weaponization of space. With the dissolution of the Soviet Union, Moscow became more open to the idea of defenses, however, primarily because its own missile defense system (which depended on radars located in the republics) was considerably degraded. Russia expressed interest in allowing missile-defense research as long as it might benefit from the results.

It can be argued that more work has been done on developing effective defenses against missiles than upgrading defenses against aircraft. If defenses are to be considered in the future as an enticement for nations not to proliferate, they must also be secure against aircraft. This text will not posit the merits of one type of air defense over another but will suggest that the opportunity exists to trade offenses—nuclear weapons, for example—for defenses.

The reason for considering defenses as a subsection of this chapter on security assurances is that some aspects of air defenses will not be transferable. That is, control over much of the technology and its operation would be kept in the hands of the designer. This is necessary for at least two reasons. First, the technical expertise required to operate the defense systems will be high-level, entailing significant training of experts in a variety of functions. Second, the technology must not be allowed to fall into the hands of those it is designed to deter because they can develop countermeasures to defeat it.

Conclusion

The role of negative security assurances in preventing nuclear proliferation is unclear. Positive security assurances that extend a nuclear umbrella by the United States or the former Soviet Union have proven to be effective nonproliferation tools. In the future, they are less likely to be useful for a number of reasons, including the unpopularity of assigning new roles to nuclear weapons. Use of advanced conventional weaponry by the United States to extend security assurances is not likely to be successful because conventional weaponry does not have the destructive power and fear element that weapons of mass destruction do. Furthermore, launching conventional capabilities is expensive, time consuming, and potentially risks more lives of the security provider.

Defenses against delivery systems might provide a disincentive to proliferate. The technology would have to be proven so that it would provide high confidence to the nation being protected. Defenses would avoid some of the high costs associated with security assurances involving either nuclear or conventional umbrellas.

Notes

1. Leonard S. Spector, "Repentant Nuclear Proliferants," *Foreign Policy,* Fall, 1992, p. 27.

2. R. Jeffrey Smith, "North Korea Gets More Time to Accept Nuclear Inspections," *The Washington Post,* February 26, 1993, p. A29.

3. Leonard S. Spector with Jacqueline R. Smith, *Nuclear Ambitions* (Boulder, CO: Westview Press, 1990) p. 60.

4. Based on input by Paul Chrzanowski to a draft of this chapter.

5. Department of Defense, Office of Comptroller, National Defense Budget Estimates for FY1993, (Washington DC, Goverment Printing Office) March, 1992, p. 142.

11

The Education Option

The most effective way to prevent nuclear proliferation is to remove a nation's motivation to acquire such weapons. The nation must be convinced that its interests are better served by not having nuclear weapons. The basic premise of this chapter is that a nation will probably not want to acquire nuclear weapons if it seriously examines the costs versus benefits. Thus, one option for discouraging nuclear proliferation is to enhance international dialog and educate nations on the disadvantages of proliferation.

The reasons for avoiding proliferation—whether it be nuclear, chemical, biological, and/or missile—ordinarily are assessed from the perspective of the international community and, more specifically, the advanced industrialized states. These countries have promoted international nonproliferation policies to avoid political instabilities and escalation of military conflicts.

When proliferation is assessed from the vantage point of the state in question, usually the focus is on what motivates that nation to want to acquire weapons of mass destruction and associated delivery systems. Generally, the state perceives that the "benefits" of proliferation are increased security, prestige, and/or political power.

As important, but less frequently discussed, is the question: Why should potential proliferants *not* want to acquire weapons of mass destruction and delivery systems? That is, how significant are the costs for the perceived benefits of weapons possession? This chapter examines some of the economic, social, security, and ecological reasons that are not in the interests of countries acquiring weapons of mass destruction and delivery systems. These issues should be made part of the discussion and debate in countries where proliferation might occur.

Economic Costs

The economic cost of acquiring and maintaining weapons of mass destruction and their delivery systems is enormous. Of course, costs will vary, depending on the type of weapon(s) chosen and the level of commitment to proper maintenance. Nuclear weapons are more expensive than chemical and biological, for example.

Developing nuclear weapons, if pursued indigenously, will cost a country billions of dollars because it entails producing special nuclear materials (e.g., plutonium or enriched uranium), nuclear device design, and high-explosives testing and manufacturing. If a device based on plutonium is chosen, for example, the facilities need a nuclear reactor, fuel fabrication and support capabilities, a plutonium-separation facility, and a high-explosives testing site.

Economic costs for nuclear weapons possession should not be estimated solely on the capital required for developing, testing, and building a small number of nuclear weapons. Other outlays should be factored in, including the investments needed for:

- Design and application of safety and security measures on the weapons, such as mechanisms to prevent accidental detonation and to assure nonusability of weapons should they fall into the hands of unauthorized users.
- Physical security for all of the facilities, equipment, nuclear materials, device designs, and other items needing protection.
- Training troops not only for nuclear weapons use but also for safe, secure transport and storage.

The facilities for research and development, testing, and manufacture of delivery systems are also expensive. In a country that does not have the established infrastructure and facilities to support missile development and manufacture, for example, the start-up costs are significant. Although a number of countries are trying to establish their own missile capabilities, virtually all of them are known to face serious technical as well as financial troubles. Some have sought to address these problems by banding together, exchanging information and/or equipment. Perhaps the most publicized example of this approach was the Condor Project among Argentina, Iraq, and Egypt—a cooperative venture that fell apart because of a variety of factors, including continuing cost problems.

Some countries have turned to imports instead of, or in addition to, indigenous production. Even this is expensive. The purchase by Syria of 150 Scud C missiles from North Korea is estimated to have cost $500 million.[1] Missiles of shorter range and lesser payload capability are less expensive but still costly. In 1990, Iraq spent over $100 million on the Astros rockets it imported from Brazil for use against Iran.[2]

In contrast to nuclear weapons and missiles or aircraft, chemical and biological weapons do not require as much capital. The production of a small arsenal is relatively inexpensive. One hundred tons of mustard gas or phosgene, for example, would cost less than $2 million to produce.[3] For more complex chemical agents, the cost would be higher, but not significantly so. For example, production of 100 tons of thionyl chloride, a principal chemical precursor for some agents, would require slightly more than $4 million. As in the case of nuclear weapons, however, looking at production costs alone is misleading. Capital will also be required to maintain safety and security of the weapons and train troops to use them.

Chemical and biological systems can be viewed as battlefield weapons having effects against which the user-soldiers conceivably can protect themselves. This would require sensors to determine the presence and concentration of a given agent, decontamination materials, and personnel protection. In the case of biological agents, for example, this might entail vaccinations against the pathogen being used. In the case of chemical agents, it would involve protective clothing and breathing apparatus. Developing and manufacturing of such sensors and protection is costly, although some effective equipment—sensors and protective gear against chemicals—may be found on the open market, making such an investment in indigenous production unnecessary.

If the country in question wishes to hide its weapons-related activities, the financial requirements will soar.[4] Facilities will need to be located underground or heavily camouflaged. Emissions will need to be masked or eliminated to prevent their detection by the growing number of detection techniques used in assuring compliance with arms-control measures. For example, Iraq built storage tanks in which to place effluents, rather than sending them to open-air ponds, to try to keep attention from its weapons programs.

Brain Drain

In countries working to build weapons of mass destruction and delivery systems, the most highly educated engineers, chemists, physicists, managers, and technicians are recruited for the weapons programs. This talent, therefore, is unavailable to develop these countries' infrastructures. In a country like the United States, where the socioeconomic and industrial infrastructure is already well established and resources are so abundant that additional talent can be developed, the impact of such a brain drain to weapons programs is not acute. In countries with lesser capabilities and resources, however, the effect is severe. There is no way to estimate the cost of nuclear proliferation to India or Pakistan, for example, but it is safe to say that the economic development of both was seriously set back by the drain of exceptional personnel to weapons development and production.

Security Costs

Ordinarily, it is assumed that a country will be more secure if it has more powerful weapons in its arsenal. It is generally believed that such weapons act to deter aggression by others and that they are more potent than conventional capabilities if deterrence fails. However, security is not always increased by acquisition of weapons of mass destruction. A country actually can be less secure in three ways upon acquiring such weapons.

Proliferants Become Targets

Upon acquiring nuclear weapons, states are more prone to be targeted by existing nuclear weapons states. Take the example of Pakistan. Before that country developed nuclear weapons, it was not subject to nuclear targeting or threat by the then-Soviet Union, United States, France, China, or the United Kingdom. All five declared nuclear weapons states had pledged not to attack any nation that itself had no nuclear weapons.[5] Pakistan is now, however, a legitimate target for the nuclear weapons of any of these countries. This "cost" of weapons ownership is not great to Pakistan now because none of the five declared nuclear weapons states have reason to attack Pakistan with nuclear weapons, but this could change in the future.

The immediate nuclear threat to Pakistan, clearly, is India's undeclared nuclear capability. Pakistan may feel that its nuclear weapons deter India, but this may also be a case wherein possession decreases rather than increases security. Pakistan cannot hope to match its potential nuclear enemies either in terms of quantity or quality of nuclear armaments. India has had at least a fourteen-year lead time to produce nuclear materials for arms. It has steadily been building a vast supply of plutonium and has established an extensive secret nuclear program that may have produced over 60 nuclear weapons.[6] The fact that Pakistan's arsenal is small relative to India's probable supply is dangerous to Pakistan not only because India can outgun it but also because there could be a greater propensity to engage nuclear weapons at an early stage of a conflict.

The greatest danger of a preemptive nuclear attack is when one side can reasonably expect to eliminate the other's nuclear forces before they can be launched. This situation is likely to occur when one side has significantly fewer nuclear weapons than the other and the location of the weapons is known. India and other nuclear weapons states know that Pakistan's arsenal must necessarily be limited in size and capability. They also know that Pakistan could be in a "use it or lose it" situation should any conflict occur. That is, if conflict starts, Pakistan will consider the possibility that India (or perhaps another nuclear weapons state) could destroy Pakistani nuclear weapons before they can be launched. Pakistan, to prevent such a preemptive strike on its limited nuclear forces, may therefore be pressured to use its nuclear weapons early and first. Meanwhile, India may be thinking that Pakistan is considering using it before losing it. India's figurative finger may thus be even closer to the trigger.

Proliferation Fuels Regional Arms Races

A nation is less secure if its neighbors and adversaries acquire weapons of mass destruction. Security is further lessened if they have the capability to deliver those weapons. Thus, it is in a nation's security interests to refrain from stimulating a regional arms race for weapons of mass destruction. And, of course, the fastest way to stimulate a regional race for nuclear, chemical, or biological weapons is for one nation within that region to acquire them.

The initiation of a race for weapons of mass destruction within a region poses more than just a security threat to the local states. It also forces nations that enter that arms race into a spiral of spending. A proliferant state that perhaps thought it could build just one or a few nuclear weapons will find itself subject to pressures to build an ever larger, more capable arsenal just to match or surpass its newly motivated competitors.

Resources Are Unavailable for Conventional Capabilities

Except in a "madman scenario" involving an irresponsible, crazy ruler, weapons of mass destruction are essentially unusable in today's world. Unlike the 1940s, when nuclear weapons were used by the United States against Japan, there is now a high level of awareness of the long-lasting effects of nuclear weapons use. Also, there probably would be strong political repercussions against the user, including severe international ostracism and sanctions. The five declared nuclear weapons states hold a common view that the primary function of nuclear weapons is to deter others who possess nuclear arsenals. They understand that nuclear war cannot be won and should not be fought.

Likewise, biological weapons are not practical. Their use may cause an epidemic that transcends borders and cannot be controlled—affecting the user as well as the initial targeted victim. Even if the user develops a vaccine against the disease it intends to use as a weapon, there is no guarantee that the weapon will not backfire. Experience with the AIDS virus, and the emergence of even stronger and less detectable strains of AIDS, has taught publics internationally the lesson that diseases respect no borders and, if mutation occurs, may become even more potent and less detectable and/or less treatable with the passage of time.

Of the three weapon types, only chemical weapons are viewed as practical and usable, yet there are some chemical agents that are extremely persistent and may pollute the environment for decades or longer. Additionally, there is a growing international norm against chemical weapons use, as is symbolized by the wide sponsorship of the Chemical Weapons Convention signed in Paris in January 1993.

If weapons are impractical or unusable, the value of having them is surely diminished. It would be better, from a military planner's perspective, to have weapons that can be used to address or forestall crises. Thus, adequate and appropriate conventional weaponry will be more useful in most situations than weapons of mass destruction (again, excepting the "madman scenario").

Constant improvements in armaments—from armor-piercing projectiles to sophisticated precision-guided munitions—make keeping up conventional capabilities a costly, difficult task. Any nation that devotes substantial resources to the development of weapons of mass destruction will probably shortchange its conventional programs. This is dangerous, and increases the probability that, in event of conflict, the nation will rely on its weapons of mass destruction. These weapons will have been developed at the expense of sufficient, effective, usable conventional military capabilities.

Environmental Damage

Dangerous, polluting substances are manufactured in the processes of making weapons of mass destruction. The United States has such serious problems with environmental damage to its nuclear-weapons-related production sites that it has had to create a multi-billion-dollar "superfund" for cleanup. The former Soviet Union has several nuclear sites so badly polluted that they should not be inhabited. One such site is near the Mayak plutonium-production plant in the Ural mountains.

The Mayak Plant began operation in 1948, and continues today. Reportedly it has caused several environmental tragedies, including:

- Radioactive waste was dumped into the nearby Techa River from 1949 to 1956, contaminating downstream areas as far away as the Ob River in far northern Siberia. Seventy-five hundred residents had to be relocated in the 1950s when the contamination became too severe in their areas and about 4000 acres remain uninhabitable.
- In 1957, there was an explosion in a radioactive-wastes storage tank that spread radioactive dust over a very large area. Approximately, 270,000 people were affected with 1200 suffering severe radiation sickness. More than 10,000 residents had to be resettled.
- Lake Karachai, near Mayak, was used as a dump for liquid radioactive waste. A drought in 1967 evaporated it, exposing radioactive sediment that was wind blown, affecting 60,000 people.[7]

The production of weapons of mass destruction and missiles to deliver them can be accomplished without pollution. To do so, however, would require enormous capital investment, more than doubling the cost of production in some cases. Almost one-half of the Department of Energy budget for the US nuclear weapons complex is devoted to cleanup, a task which could cost over $100 billion and take 30 years to complete.[8] This brings the argument back to the issue of economic cost: the trade-off is either polluted environment or a much higher financial cost for weapons.

Good for Superpowers, Good for Everyone?

Sometimes less developed countries argue that they should acquire nuclear or chemical weapons because the superpowers possess them and have derived tremendous benefit politically and militarily. In our international political system, individual sovereign nations have the freedom to pursue these as well as biological weapons and delivery systems.[9] But arguments that having such weapons is more beneficial than detrimental should be challenged.

The former Soviet Union serves as an example of what can happen when weapons programs consume a large proportion of available capital and the best talent in the nation. It is also a prime example of weapons production at the expense of the environment. In Chepayesk, a city devoted to chemicals-for-weapons production, the air and soil have dangerous levels of carcinogenic chemicals. Health of the general population is exceedingly poor. And, standard-of-living is poor; one-third of the households do not have running water. The state invested in the chemicals factories, not in social services or the economy.

Sweden examined the idea of having nuclear weapons and rejected it on the basis that it was too expensive and would not result in an increase in security. Sweden had a nuclear weapons program and then abandoned it, largely because it realized that it could never match the quality or quantity of the nuclear arsenals of the existing nuclear weapons states. Also, the Swedish Parliament debated the issue and determined that the financial cost of weapons production was unacceptably high.

Japan and Germany are also good examples of countries that have foregone the nuclear option, investing capital in their economies rather than military production capabilities. Part of their economic-superpower status can be attributed to the fact that they have not had the financial burden of weapons production and maintenance.

It also should be noted here that the United States and Russia have worked hard to reduce their arsenals. Not only have chemical and biological weapons been outlawed by both,[10] but nuclear weapons have been reduced, and an entire class of missiles has been eliminated from their stockpiles.[11] And even this process is costly. The United States is spending more than $8 billion to destroy its chemical weapons stockpile and has already allocated $800 million for the destruction of nuclear and chemical weapons of the former Soviet Union.

In conclusion, the message for potential proliferants is clear: Weapons of mass destruction and associated delivery systems are extremely expensive to make, maintain, use, and destroy. Any country contemplating proliferation should consider the profound costs of doing so.

Notes

1. Steven Emerson, "The Postwar Scud Boom," *The Wall Street Journal*, July 10, 1991, p. 12

2. *The Financial Times*, September 10, 1990.

3. Kathleen Bailey et al., *Noncompliance Scenarios: Means By Which Parties to the Chemical Weapons Convention Might Cheat*, study completed for Defense Nuclear Agency contract DNA 001-90-C-0173, January, 1992, pp. 28-29.

4. This point is not a significant problem with biological-agent production because there are few, if any, emissions that can be detected, and there are no distinguishing features which might make illicit production of pathogens more readily detectable. Also, the space requirements are exceedingly small; an average-size room will do.

5. The exact language of these pledges varies. For example, the United States declares that countries also must not be allied with a nuclear weapons state in order to qualify for the negative security assurance.

6. This figure is based on a study by the Stockholm International Peace Research Institute, as reported in Johan Rapp, "Institute Keeps Tabs On Weapons Material," *The Washington Times*, March 2, 1993, p. A8.

7. "Russian Government Plans," UPI story carried on Mainstream Newscast Database, January 27, 1993.

8. Jon Christensen, "Deep Freeze," *Metro* (San Jose, CA) December 10, 1992.

9. An exception to this is the case of Iraq. The United Nations resolved that Iraq must declare and destroy its weapons of mass destruction and missiles.

10. There is evidence that Russia has continued not only its chemical-weapons programs, but its biological weapons research as well, despite its commitments to abandon both. See US Arms Control & Disarmament Agency, "Adherence To and Compliance with Arms Control Agreements and The President's Report to Congress on Soviet Noncompliance with Arms Control Agreements" January 14, 1993, pp. 13-14.

11. The 1987 Intermediate Nuclear Forces Treaty eliminated all ground-launched ballistic missiles with ranges of 500 to 5500 kilometers.

12

Conclusion

The nuclear nonproliferation regime has slowed the spread of nuclear weapons and weapons technology, but it has not and cannot stop proliferation by a determined nation. The regime—whose primary components are treaties, export controls, and diplomatic activities by individual nations—has always faced obstacles such as nonparticipation by key countries and noncompliance by a few regime participants.

In the future, the nuclear nonproliferation regime will face more challenges than it has in the past. The "traditional" problem of weapons acquisition by technologically less-advanced countries is joined by a new phenomenon, proliferation resulting from the breakup of a nuclear weapons state, the USSR. Also, the vulnerability of the Nuclear Nonproliferation Treaty (NPT) to cheating has been demonstrated by Iraq and North Korea. North Korea has announced withdrawal from the NPT and, if it follows through, will shake member-parties' confidence that the treaty is a meaningful barrier to proliferation.

In 1995, participating nations will decide for how long the NPT should be extended. Parties to the treaty will have to evaluate whether they are more secure with the NPT than without, and whether the treaty should be changed in any way. Several nations and subnational interest groups will probably try to alter the NPT to achieve their own goals. For example, opponents of nuclear testing may try to add a protocol to require a comprehensive test ban.

Although the nuclear nonproliferation regime has serious deficiencies, the challenges it is facing and will face in the near term should not be allowed to undermine or radically change the basic building blocks of the regime. Attempts to change the NPT, for example, would probably result in a large array of proposals for additions, deletions, and protocols. This could dilute the NPT or increase the rigor of its language, possibly making it unacceptable to some current and potential parties. Similarly, attempts to alter export controls can backfire. For example, bringing second-tier suppliers into the Nuclear Suppliers Group may free high-technology exports to these countries. While these countries will be restricted from re-exporting the imports, the technologies will make their own weapons capabilities stronger.

The goal for 1995 and thereafter should not be merely to extend an unaltered NPT but rather to increase the demands for and participation in arms control and nonproliferation worldwide. There should be increased emphasis on:

- Improving the safeguards regime,
- Developing detection and verification technologies,
- Providing security assurances when feasible, and
- Educating publics and governments on the costs and problems associated with nuclear weapons possession.

Additionally, there are policy options listed below that have been somewhat successful in the past and could be applied in some circumstances and cases in the future.

Focus on Regional Conflict Resolution

Regional conflicts, often the source of motives to acquire ever more powerful weaponry, must be addressed on a case-by-case basis. This approach has led to positive results in at least two instances:

- The Argentina–Brazil agreement to increase transparency of one another's nuclear programs, and
- The North and South Korean agreement to make the peninsula a nuclear-weapons-free zone and to forgo production of special nuclear materials usable in weapons.

Although it can be argued that nuclear proliferation has not been foreclosed in either Latin America or on the Korean Peninsula, these agreements constitute significant progress toward transparency and confidence building. The regional approach has also been tried in South Asia and the Middle East, thus far with little success. Efforts to resolve conflicts in these regions should continue, and any solutions proposed should address proliferation.

Widen Participation in Arms Control Agreements

A central concern of nuclear nonproliferation policy should be delivery systems. Although it is possible to deliver a nuclear device via clandestine means, such as using a commercial ship or truck, only one or a few nuclear weapons can be delivered this way. Also, clandestine delivery is likely to be time consuming and would therefore be less useful in a conflict requiring quick response. In quick-response scenarios, nations are likely to want the capability to deliver their nuclear weapons either by aircraft or missile. For this reason, it is disturbing that many of the countries suspected of developing weapons of mass destruction are also acquiring air-delivery capabilities.

The United States and Soviet Union recognized that delivery systems enhance nuclear threats, yet they are more easily controlled than nuclear warheads. For this reason, the United States and Soviet Union negotiated the Intermediate Nuclear Force Treaty (INF) to ban from their arsenals all ground-launched ballistic and cruise missiles capable of traveling 500 to 5500 kilometers. It would make sense to expand membership in the INF Treaty or to create an international INF. The arms-control progress made by the United States and Soviet Union on limiting delivery systems should be expanded to other countries. Wider adherence in some other arms-control agreements should be sought as well. For example, other nuclear weapons states should become party to nuclear-test-limitation treaties.

Military Intervention Should Be Considered

When Israel bombed the Iraqi nuclear reactor in June 1981, it set back Iraq's nuclear weapons ambitions. Even though military action can be successful in limiting or eliminating a country's nuclear program, dangers are involved. For example, nuclear materials can be spread, contaminating large areas downwind. And even if there are no nuclear dangers, such an attack can lead to a large-scale military conflict. Nevertheless, the possibility of a military strike—by a single nation, set of nations, or the international community—should be considered in cases where proliferation presents a clear threat to international stability and other means to solve the problem have failed.

Even if military action is used and results in setting back a country's nuclear program, the setback may be only temporary, as it was in the case of Iraq. Use of force is unlikely to change a country's motivations to acquire nuclear weapons, and in fact may stiffen that resolve.

In conclusion, policies that focus on denial—whether by force, technology controls, or laws—cannot stop nuclear proliferation. The best solution is to find ways to change nations' motivations, to help them decide for themselves that nuclear weapons possession is not in their best interests.

APPENDIX A

United Nations Security Council Resolution 687 (1991)

The Security Council,

Recalling its resolutions 660 (1990) of 2 August 1990, 661 (1990) of 6 August 1990, 662 (1990) of 9 August 1990, 664 (1990) of 18 August 1990, 665 (1990) of 25 August 1990, 666 (1990) of 13 September 1990, 667 (1990) of 16 September 1990, 669 (1990) of 24 September 1990, 670 (1990) of 25 September 1990, 674 (1990) of 29 October 1990, 677 (1990) of 28 November 1990, 678 (1990) of 29 November 1990 and 686 (1991) of 2 March 1991,

Welcoming the restoration to Kuwait of its sovereignty, independence and territorial integrity and the return of its legitimate Government,

Affirming the commitment of all Member States to the sovereignty, territorial integrity and political independence of Kuwait and Iraq, and noting the intention expressed by the Member States cooperating with Kuwait under paragraph 2 of resolution 678 (1990) to bring their military presence in Iraq to an end as soon as possible consistent with paragraph 8 of resolution 686 (1991),

Reaffirming the need to be assured of Iraq's peaceful intentions in the light of its unlawful invasion and occupation of Kuwait,

Taking note of the letter sent by the Minister for Foreign Affairs of Iraq on 27 February 1991 and those sent pursuant to resolution 686 (1991),

Noting that Iraq and Kuwait, as independent sovereign States, signed at Baghdad on 4 October 1963 "Agreed Minutes Between the State of Kuwait and the Republic of Iraq Regarding the Restoration of Friendly Relations, Recognition and Related Matters", thereby recognizing formally the boundary between Iraq and Kuwait and the allocation of islands, which were registered with the United Nations in accordance with Article 102 of the Charter of the United Nations and in which Iraq recognized the independence and complete sovereignty of the State of Kuwait within its borders as specified and accepted in the letter of the Prime Minister of Iraq dated 21

July 1932, and as accepted by the Ruler of Kuwait in his letter dated 10 August 1932,

Conscious of the need for demarcation of the said boundary,

Conscious also of the statements by Iraq threatening to use weapons in violation of its obligations under the Geneva Protocol for the Prohibition of the Use in War of Asphyxiating, Poisonous or Other Gases, and of Bacteriological Methods of Warfare, signed at Geneva on 17 June 1925, and of its prior use of chemical weapons and affirming that grave consequences would follow any further use by Iraq of such weapons,

Recalling that Iraq has subscribed to the Declaration adopted by all States participating in the Conference of States Parties to the 1925 Geneva Protocol and Other Interested States, held in Paris from 7 to 11 January 1989, establishing the objective of universal elimination of chemical and biological weapons,

Recalling also that Iraq has signed the Convention on the prohibition of the Development, Production and Stockpiling of Bacteriological (Biological) and Toxin Weapons and on their Destruction, of 10 April 1972,

Noting the importance of Iraq ratifying this Convention,

Noting moreover the importance of all States adhering to this Convention and encouraging its forthcoming Review Conference to reinforce the authority, efficiency and universal scope of the Convention,

Stressing the importance of an early conclusion by the Conference on Disarmament of its work on a Convention on the Universal Prohibition of Chemical Weapons and of universal adherence thereto,

Aware of the use by Iraq of ballistic missiles in unprovoked attacks and therefore of the need to take specific measures in regard to such missiles located in Iraq,

Concerned by the reports in the hands of Member States that Iraq has attempted to acquire materials for a nuclear-weapons programme contrary to its obligations under the Treaty on the Non-Proliferation of Nuclear Weapons of 1 July 1968,

Recalling the objective of the establishment of a nuclear-weapons-free zone in the region of the Middle East,

Conscious of the threat that all weapons of mass destruction pose to peace and security in the area and of the need to work towards the establishment in the Middle East of a zone free of such weapons,

Conscious also of the objective of achieving balanced and comprehensive control of armaments in the region,

Conscious further of the importance of achieving the objectives noted above using all available means, including a dialogue among the States of the region,

Noting that resolution 686 (1991) marked the lifting of the measures imposed by resolution 661 (1990) in so far as they applied to Kuwait,

Noting that despite the progress being made in fulfilling the obligations of resolution 686 (1991), many Kuwaiti and third country nationals are still not accounted for and property remains unreturned,

Recalling the International Convention against the Taking of Hostages, opened for signature at New York on 18 December 1979, which categorizes all acts of taking hostages as manifestations of international terrorism,

Deploring threats made by Iraq during the recent conflict to make use of terrorism against targets outside Iraq and the taking of hostages by Iraq,

Taking note with grave concern of the reports of the Secretary General of 20 March 1991 and 28 March 1991, and conscious of the necessity to meet urgently the humanitarian needs in Kuwait and Iraq,

Bearing in mind its objective of restoring international peace and security in the area as set out in recent resolutions of the Security Council,

Conscious of the need to take the following measures acting under Chapter VII of: the Charter,

1. Affirms all thirteen resolutions noted above, except as expressly changed below to achieve the goals of this resolution, including a formal cease-fire;

A

2. Demands that Iraq and Kuwait respect the inviolability of the international boundary and the allocation of islands set out in the "Agreed Minutes Between the State of Kuwait and the Republic of Iraq

Regarding the Restoration of Friendly Relations, Recognition and Related Matters", signed by them in the exercise of their sovereignty at Baghdad on 4 October 1963 and registered with the United Nations and published by the United Nations in document 7063, United Nations, *Treaty Series*, 1964;

3. Calls upon the Secretary-General to lend his assistance to make arrangements with Iraq and Kuwait to demarcate the boundary between Iraq and Kuwait, drawing on appropriate material, including the map transmitted by Security Council document S/22412 and to report back to the Security Council within one month;

4. Decides to guarantee the inviolability of the above-mentioned international boundary and to take as appropriate all necessary measures to that end in accordance with the Charter of the United Nations;

B

5. Requests the Secretary-General, after consulting with Iraq and Kuwait, to submit within three days to the Security Council for its approval a plan for the immediate deployment of a United Nations observer unit to monitor the Khor Abdullah and a demilitarized zone, which is hereby established, extending ten kilometres into Iraq and five kilometres into Kuwait from the boundary referred to in the "Agreed Minutes Between the State of Kuwait and the Republic of Iraq Regarding the Restoration of Friendly Relations, Recognition and Related Matters" of 4 October 1963; to deter violations of the boundary through its presence in and surveillance of the demilitarized zone; to observe any hostile or potentially hostile action mounted from the territory of one State to the other, and for the Secretary-General to report regularly to the Security Council on the operations of the unit, and immediately if there are serious violations of the zone or potential threats to peace;

6. Notes that as soon as the Secretary-General notifies the Security Council of the completion of the deployment of the United Nations observer unit, the conditions will be established for the Member States cooperating with Kuwait in accordance with resolution 678 (1990) to bring their military presence in Iraq to an end consistent with resolution 686 (1991);

C

7. <u>Invites</u> Iraq to reaffirm unconditionally its obligations under the Geneva Protocol for the Prohibition of the Use in War of Asphyxiating, Poisonous or Other Gases, and of Bacteriological Methods of Warfare, signed at Geneva on 17 June 1925, and to ratify the Convention on the Prohibition of the Development, Production and Stockpiling of Bacteriological (Biological) and Toxin Weapons and on Their Destruction, of 10 April 1972;

8. <u>Decides</u> that Iraq shall unconditionally accept the destruction, removal, or rendering harmless, under international supervision, of:

   (a) All chemical and biological weapons and all stocks of agents and all related subsystems and components and all research, development, support and manufacturing facilities;

   (b) All ballistic missiles with a range greater than 150 kilometres and related major parts, and repair and production facilities;

9. <u>Decides</u>, for the implementation of paragraph 8 above, the following:

   (a) Iraq shall submit to the Secretary-General, within fifteen days of the adoption of the present resolution, a declaration of the locations, amounts and types of all items specified in paragraph 8 and agree to urgent, on-site inspection as specified below;

   (b) The Secretary-General, in consultation with the appropriate Governments and, where appropriate, with the Director-General of the World Health Organization, within forty-five days of the Passage of the present resolution, shall develop, and submit to the Council for approval, a plan calling for the completion of the following acts within forty-five days of such approval:

   (i) The forming of a Special Commission, which shall carry out immediate on-site inspection of Iraq's biological, chemical and missile capabilities, based on Iraq's declarations and the designation of any additional locations by the Special Commission itself;

   (ii) The yielding by Iraq of possession to the Special commission for destruction, removal or rendering harmless, taking into account the requirements of public safety, of all items specified under paragraph 8 (a) above, including items at the additional locations designated by the Special Commission under paragraph 9 (b) (i) above and the destruction by Iraq, under the supervision of the Special Commission, of all its missile capabilities, including launchers, as specified under paragraph 8 (b) above;

(iii) The provision by the Special Commission of the assistance and cooperation to the Director-General of the International Atomic Energy Agency required in paragraphs 12 and 13 below:

10. Decides that Iraq shall unconditionally undertake not to use, develop, construct or acquire any of the items specified in paragraphs 8 and 9 above and requests the Secretary-General, in consultation with the Special Commission, to develop a plan for the future ongoing monitoring and verification of Iraq's compliance with this paragraph, to be submitted to the Security Council for approval within one hundred and twenty days of the passage of this resolution:

11. Invites Iraq to reaffirm unconditionally its obligations under the 'Treaty on the Non-Proliferation of Nuclear Weapons of I July 1968;

12. Decides that Iraq shall unconditionally agree not to acquire or develop nuclear weapons or nuclear-weapons-usable material or any subsystems or components or any research, development, support or manufacturing facilities related to the above; to submit to the Secretary-General and the Director-General of the International Atomic Energy Agency within fifteen days of the adoption of the present resolution a declaration of the locations, amounts, and types of all items specified above; to place all of its nuclear-weapons-usable materials under the exclusive control, for custody and removal, of the International Atomic Energy Agency, with the assistance and cooperation of the Special Commission as provided for in the plan of the Secretary-General discussed in paragraph 9 (b) above; to accept, in accordance with the arrangements provided for in paragraph 13 below, urgent on-site inspection and the destruction, removal or rendering harmless as appropriate of all items specified above; and to accept the plan discussed in paragraph 13 below for the future ongoing monitoring and verification of its compliance with these undertakings;

13. Requests the Director-General of the International Atomic Energy Agency, through the Secretary-General, with the assistance and cooperation of the Special Commission as provided for in the plan of the Secretary-General in paragraph 9 (b) above, to carry out immediate on-site inspection of Iraq's nuclear capabilities based on Iraq's declarations and the designation of any additional locations by the Special Commission; to develop a plan for submission to the Security Council within forty-five days calling for the destruction, removal, or rendering harmless as appropriate of all items listed in paragraph 12 above; to carry out the plan within forty-five days following approval by the Security Council; and to develop a plan, taking into account the rights and obligations of Iraq under the Treaty on the Non-Proliferation of Nuclear Weapons of 1 July 1968, for the future ongoing monitoring and verification of Iraq's compliance with paragraph 12 above, including an inventory of all nuclear material in Iraq subject to the Agency's verification and inspections of the international Atomic Energy Agency to confirm that the Agency's safeguards cover all relevant nuclear activities in Iraq, to be submitted to the Security Council for approval within one hundred and twenty days of the passage of the present resolution;

14 Takes note that the actions to be taken by Iraq in paragraphs 8, 9, 10, 11, 12 and 13 of the present resolution represent steps towards the goal of establishing in the Middle East a zone free from weapons of mass destruction and all missiles for their delivery and the objective of a global ban on chemical weapons;

D

15. Requests the Secretary-General to report to the Security Council on the steps taken to facilitate the return of all Kuwaiti property seized by Iraq, including a list of any property that Kuwait claims has not been returned or which has not been returned intact;

E

16. Reaffirms that Iraq, without prejudice to the debts and obligations of Iraq arising prior to 2 August 1990, which will be addressed through the nominal mechanisms, is liable under international law for any direct loss, damage, including environmental damage and the depletion of natural resources, or injury to foreign Governments, nationals

and corporations, as a result of Iraq's unlawful invasion and occupation of Kuwait;

17. Decides that all Iraqi statements made since 2 August 1990 repudiat-
ing its foreign debt are null and void, and demands that Iraq adhere
scrupulously to all of its obligations concerning servicing and repay-
ment of its foreign debt;

18. Decides also to create a fund to pay compensation for claims that fall
within , paragraph 16 above and to establish a Commission that will
administer the fund;

19. Directs the Secretary-General to develop and present to the Security
Council for decision, no later than thirty days following the adoption
of the present resolution, recommendations for the fund to meet the
requirement for the payment of claims established in accordance with
paragraph 18 above and for a programme to implement the decisions
in paragraphs 16, 17 and 18 above, including: administration of the
fund; mechanisms for determining the appropriate level of Iraq's
contribution to the fund based on a percentage of the value of the
exports of petroleum and petroleum products from Iraq not to exceed
a figure to be suggested to the Council by the Secretary-General,
taking into account the requirements of the people of Iraq, Iraq's
payment capacity as assessed in conjunction with the international
financial institutions taking into consideration external debt service,
and the needs of the Iraqi economy; arrangements for ensuring that
payments are made to the fund; the process by which funds will be
allocated and claims paid; appropriate procedures for evaluating
losses, listing claims and verifying their validity and resolving dis-
puted claims in respect of Iraq's liability as specified in paragraph 16
above; and the composition of the Commission designated above;

F

20. Decides, effective immediately, that the prohibitions against the sale
or supply to Iraq of commodities or products, other than medicine
and health supplies, and prohibitions against financial transactions
related thereto contained in resolution 661 (1990) shall not apply to
foodstuffs notified to the Security Council Committee established by
resolution 661 (1990) concerning the situation between Iraq and
Kuwait or, with the approval of that Committee, under the simplified
and accelerated "no-objection" procedure, to materials and supplies
for essential civilian needs as identified in the report of the Secretary-

General dated 20 March 1991, and in any further findings of humanitarian need by the Committee;

21. Decides that the Security Council shall review the provisions of paragraph 20 above every sixty days in the light of the policies and practices of the Government of Iraq, including the implementation of all relevant resolutions of the Security Council, for the purpose of determining whether to reduce or lift the prohibitions referred to therein;

22. Decides that upon the approval by the Security Council of the programme called for in paragraph 19 above and upon Council agreement that Iraq has completed all actions contemplated in paragraphs 8, 9, 10, 11, 12 and 13 above, the prohibitions against the import of commodities and products originating in Iraq and the prohibitions against financial transactions related thereto contained in resolution 661 (1990) shall have no further force or effect;

23. Decides that, pending action by the Security Council under paragraph 22 above, the Security Council Committee established by resolution 661 (1990) shall be empowered to approve, when required to assure adequate financial resources on the part of Iraq to carry out the activities under paragraph 20 above, exceptions to the prohibition against the import of commodities and products originating in Iraq;

24. Decides that, in accordance with resolution 661 (1990) and subsequent related resolutions and until a further decision is taken by the Security Council, all States shall continue to prevent the sale or supply, or the promotion or facilitation of such sale or supply, to Iraq by their nationals, or from then territories or using their flag vessels or aircraft, of:

(a) Arms and related *materiel* of all types, specifically including the sale or transfer through other means of all forms of conventional military equipment, including for paramilitary forces, and spare parts and components and their means of production, for such equipment;

(b) Items specified and defined in paragraphs 8 and 12 above not otherwise covered above;

(c) Technology under licensing or other transfer arrangements used in the production, utilization or stockpiling of items specified in subparagraphs (a) and (b) above;

   (d) Personnel or materials for training or technical support services relating to the design, development, manufacture, use, maintenance or support of items specified in subparagraphs (a) and (b) above;

25. Calls upon all States and international organizations to act strictly in accordance with paragraph 24 above, notwithstanding the existence of any contracts, agreements, licenses or any other arrangements;

26. Requests the Secretary-General, in consultation with appropriate Governments, to develop within sixty days, for the approval of the Security Council, guidelines to facilitate full international implementation of paragraphs 24 and 25 above and paragraph 27 below, and to make them available to all States and to establish a procedure for updating these guidelines periodically;

27. Calls upon all States to maintain such national controls and procedures and to take such other actions consistent with the guidelines to be established by the Security Council under paragraph 26 above as may be necessary to ensure compliance with the terms of paragraph 24 above, and calls upon international organizations to take all appropriate steps to assist in ensuring such full compliance;

28. Agrees to review its decisions in paragraphs 22, 23, 24 and 25 above, except for the items specified and defined in paragraphs 8 and 12 above, on a regular basis and in any case one hundred and twenty days following passage of the present resolution, taking into account Iraq's compliance with the resolution and general progress towards the control of armaments in the region;

29. Decides that all States, including Iraq, shall take the necessary measures to ensure that no claim shall lie at the instance of the Government of Iraq, or of any person or body in Iraq, or of any person claiming through or for the benefit of any such person or body, in connection with any contract or other transaction where its performance was affected by reason of the measures taken by the Security Council in resolution 661 (1990) and related resolutions;

G

30. Decides that, in furtherance of its commitment to facilitate the repatriation of all Kuwaiti and third country nationals, Iraq shall extend all necessary cooperation to the international Committee of the Red

Cross, providing lists of such persons, facilitating the access of the International Committee of the Red Cross to all such persons wherever located or detained and facilitating the search by the International Committee of the Red Cross for those Kuwaiti and third country nationals still unaccounted for,

31. Invites the International Committee of the Red Cross to keep the Secretary-General apprised as appropriate of all activities undertaken in connection with facilitating the repatriation or return of all Kuwaiti and third country nationals or their remains present in Iraq on or after 2 August 1990;

H

32. Requires Iraq to inform the Security Council that it will not commit or support any act of international terrorism or allow any organization directed towards commission of such acts to operate within its territory and to condemn unequivocally and renounce all acts, methods and practices of terrorism;

33. Declares that, upon official notification by Iraq to the Secretary-General and to the Security Council of its acceptance of the provisions above, a formal cease-fire is effective between Iraq and Kuwait and the Member States cooperating with Kuwait in accordance with resolution 678 (1990);

34. Decides to remain seized of the matter and to take such further steps as may be required for the implementation of the present resolution and to secure peace and security in the area.

APPENDIX B

United Nations Security Council Resolution 707 (1991)

The Security Council,

Recalling its resolution 687 (1991), and its other resolutions on this matter,

Recalling the letter of 11 April 1991 from the President of the Security Council to the Permanent Representative of Iraq to the United Nations (S/22485) noting that on the basis Of Iraq's written agreement (S/22456) to implement fully resolution 687 (1991) the preconditions established in paragraph 33 of that resolution for a cease-fire had been met,

Noting with grave concern the letters dated 26 June 1991 (S/22739), 28 June 1991 (S/22743) and 4 July 1991 (S/22761) from the Secretary-General, conveying information obtained from the Executive Chairman of the Special Commission and the Director-General of the IAEA which establishes Iraq's failure to comply with its obligations under resolution 687 (1991),

Recalling further the statement issued by the President of the Security Council on 28 June 1991 (S/22746) requesting that a high-level mission consisting of the Chairman of the Special Commission, the Director-General of the IAEA, and the Under-Secretary-General for Disarmament Affairs be dispatched to meet with officials at the highest levels of the Government of Iraq at the earliest opportunity to obtain written assurance that Iraq will fully and immediately cooperate in the inspection of the locations identified by the Special Commission and present for immediate inspection any of those items that may have been transported from those locations,

Dismayed by the report of the-high-level mission to the Secretary-General (S/22761) on the results of its meetings with the highest levels of the Iraqi Government,

Gravely concerned by the information provided to the Council by the Special Commission and the IAEA on 15 July 1991 (S/22788) and 25 July 1991 (S/22837) regarding the actions of the Government of Iraq in flagrant violation of resolution 687 (1991),

Gravely concerned also by the evidence in the letter of 7 July 1991 from the minister of Foreign Affairs of Iraq to the Secretary-General and in subsequent statements and findings that Iraq's notifications of 18 and 28 April were incomplete and that it had concealed activities, which both constituted material breaches of its obligations under resolution 687 (1991),

Noting also from the letters dated 26 June 1991 (S/22739), 28 June 1991 (S/22743) and 4 July 1991 (S/22761) from the Secretary-General that Iraq has not fully complied with all of its undertakings relating to the privileges, immunities and facilities to be accorded to the Special Commission and the IAEA inspection teams mandated under resolution 687 (1991),

Affirming that in order for the Special Commission to carry out its mandate under paragraph 9 (b) (i), (ii) and (iii) of resolution 687 (1991) to inspect Iraq's chemical and biological weapons and ballistic missile capabilities and to take possession of them for destruction, removal or rendering harmless, full disclosure on the part of Iraq as required in paragraph 9 (a) of resolution 687 (1991) is essential,

Affirming that in order for the IAEA, with the assistance and cooperation of the Special Commission, to determine what nuclear-weapons-usable material or any subsystems or components or any research, development, support or manufacturing facilities related to them need, in accordance with paragraph 13 of resolution 687 (1991), to be destroyed, removed or rendered harmless, Iraq is required to make a declaration of all its nuclear programmes including any which it claims are for purposes not related to nuclear-weapons-usable material,

Affirming that the aforementioned failures of Iraq to act in strict conformity with its obligations under resolution 687 (1991) constitutes a material breach of its acceptance of the relevant provisions of resolution 687 (1991) which established a cease-fire and provided the conditions essential to the restoration of peace and security in the region,

Affirming further that Iraq's failure to comply with its safeguards agreement with the International Atomic Energy Agency, concluded pursuant to the Treaty on the Non-Proliferation of Nuclear Weapons of 1 July 1968, as established by the resolution of the Board of Governors of the IAEA of 18 July 1991 (GOV/2532),* constitutes a breach of its international obligations,

Determined to ensure full compliance with resolution 687 (1991) and in particular its section C,

Acting under Chapter VII of the Charter,

1. Condemns Iraq's serious violation of a number of its obligations under section C of resolution 687 (1991) and of its undertakings to cooperate with the Special Commission and the IAEA, which constitutes a material breach of the relevant provisions of resolution 687 which established a cease-fire and provided the conditions essential to the restoration of peace and security in the region;

2. Further condemns non-compliance by the Government of Iraq with its obligations under its safeguards agreement with the International Atomic Energy Agency, as established by the resolution of the Board of Governors of 18 July, which constitutes a violation of its commitments as a party to the Treaty on the Non-Proliferation of Nuclear Weapons of 1 July 1968;

3. Demands that Iraq

(i) provide full, final and complete disclosure, as required by resolution 687 (1991), of all aspects of its programmes to develop weapons of mass destruction and ballistic missiles with a range greater than 150 km, and of all holdings of such weapons, their components and production facilities and locations, as well as all other nuclear programmes, including any which it claims are for purposes not related to nuclear-weapons-usable material, without further delay;

(ii) allow the Special Commission, the IAEA and their Inspection Teams immediate, unconditional and unrestricted access to any and all areas, facilities, equipment, records and means of transportation which they wish to inspect;

(iii) cease immediately any attempt to conceal, or any movement or destruction of any material or equipment relating to its nuclear, chemical or biological weapons or ballistic missile programmes, or material or equipment relating to its other nuclear activities without notification to and prior consent of the Special Commission;

(iv) make available immediately to the Special Commission, the IAEA and their Inspection Teams any items to which they were previously denied access;

(v) allow the Special Commission, the IAEA and their Inspection Teams to conduct both fixed wing and helicopter flights throughout Iraq for all relevant purposes including inspection, surveillance, aerial

surveys, transportation and logistics without interference of any kind
and upon such terms and conditions as may be determined by the
Special Commission, and to make full use of their own aircraft and
such airfields in Iraq as they may determine are most appropriate for
the work of the Commission;

(vi) halt all nuclear activities of any kind, except for use of isotopes for
medical, agricultural or industrial purposes until the Security Council
determines that Iraq is in full compliance with this resolution and
paragraphs 12 and 13 of resolution 687 (1991), and the IAEA determines
that Iraq is in full compliance with its safeguards agreement with that
Agency;

(vii) ensure the complete implementation of the privileges, immunities and facilities of the representatives of the Special Commission and
the IAEA in accordance with its previous undertakings and their
complete safety and freedom of movement;

(viii) immediately provide or facilitate the provision of any transportation, medical or logistical support requested by the Special Commission, the IAEA and their Inspection Teams;

(ix) respond fully, completely and promptly to any questions or
requests from the Special Commission, the IAEA and their Inspection
Teams;

4. Determines that Iraq retains no ownership interest in items to be
   destroyed, removed or rendered harmless pursuant to paragraph 12
   of resolution 687 (1991);

5. Requires that the Government of Iraq forthwith comply fully and
   without delay with all its international obligations, including those
   set out in the present resolution, in resolution 687 (1991), in the Treaty
   on the Non-Proliferation of Nuclear Weapons of 1 July 1968 and its
   safeguards agreement with the IAEA;

6. Decides to remain seized of this matter.

*A/45/1037; S/22812, appendix.

APPENDIX C

United Nations Security Council Resolution 715 (1991)

The Security Council,

Recalling its resolutions 687 (1991) of 3 April 1991 and 707 (1991) of 15 August 1991, and its other resolutions on this matter,

Recalling in particular that under resolution 687 (1991) the Secretary-General and the Director General of the International Atomic Energy Agency were requested to develop plans for future ongoing monitoring and verification, and to submit them to the Security Council for approval,

Taking note of the report and note of the Secretary-General, * transmitting the plans submitted by the Secretary-General and the Director General of the International Atomic Energy Agency,

Acting under Chapter VII of the Charter of the United Nations,

1. Approves, in accordance with the provisions of resolutions 687 (1991), 707 (1991) and the present resolution, the plans submitted by the Secretary-General and the Director General of the International Atomic Energy Agency;*

2. Decides that the Special Commission shall carry out the plan submitted by the Secretary-General,[†] as well as continuing to discharge its other responsibilities under resolutions 687 (1991), 699 (1991) and 707 (1991) and performing such other functions as are conferred upon it under the present resolution;

3. Requests the Director General of the International Atomic Energy Agency to carry out, with the assistance and cooperation of the Special Commission, the plan submitted by him[§] and to continue to discharge his other responsibilities under resolutions 687 (1991), 699 (1991) and 707 (1991);

4. Decides that the Special Commission, in the exercise of its responsibilities as a subsidiary organ of the Security Council, shall:

   (a) Continue to have the responsibility for designating additional
       locations for inspection and overflights;

   (b) Continue to render assistance and cooperation to the Director
       General of the International Atomic Energy Agency, by provid-
       ing him by mutual agreement with the necessary special exper-
       tise and logistical, informational and other operational support
       for the carrying out of the plan submitted by him;

   (c) Perform such other functions, in cooperation in the nuclear field
       with the Director General of the International Atomic Energy
       Agency, as may be necessary to coordinate activities under the
       plans approved by the present resolution, including making use
       of commonly available services and information to the fullest
       extent possible, in order to achieve maximum efficiency and
       optimum use of resources;

5. Demands that Iraq meet unconditionally all its obligations under the
   plans approved by the present resolution and cooperate fully with
   the Special commission and the Director General of the International
   Atomic Energy Agency in carrying out the plans;

6. Decides to encourage the maximum assistance, in cash and in kind,
   from all Member States to support the Special Commission and the
   Director General of the International Atomic Energy Agency in
   carrying out their activities under the plans approved by the present
   resolution, without prejudice to Iraq's liability for the full costs of
   such activities;

7. Requests the Committee established under resolution 661 (1990), the
   Special Commission and the Director General of the International
   Atomic Energy Agency to develop in cooperation a mechanism for
   monitoring any future sales or supplies by other countries to Iraq of
   items relevant to the implementation of section C of resolution 687
   (1991) and other relevant resolutions, including the present resolution and the plans approved hereunder,

8. Requests the Secretary-General and the Director General of the
   International Atomic Energy Agency to submit to the Security Council reports on the implementation of the plans approved by the

present resolution, when requested by the Security Council and in any event at least every six months after the adoption of this resolution;

9. <u>Decides</u> to remain seized of the matter.

*S/22871/Rev.1 and S/22872/Rev. 1 and Corr.1
†S/22871/Rev.1
§S/22872/Rev.1 and Corr.1.

Acronyms

CTB	Comprehensive Test Ban
EC	European Community
EMIS	Electromagnetic Isotope Separation
IAEA	International Atomic Energy Agency
INF	Intermediate Nuclear Forces Treaty
MBAs	Material Balance Areas
NATO	North Atlantic Treaty Organization
NPT	Nuclear Nonproliferation Treaty
START	Strategic Arms Reduction Treaty
UNSCOM	United Nations Special Commission
UNSCR	United Nations Security Council Resolution

Index